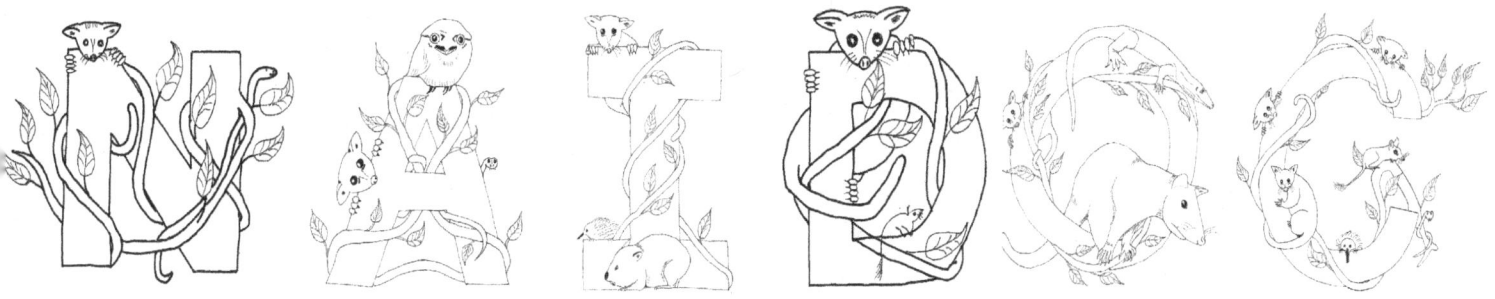

Wanaruah
NAIDOC Colouring Book
Volume 1

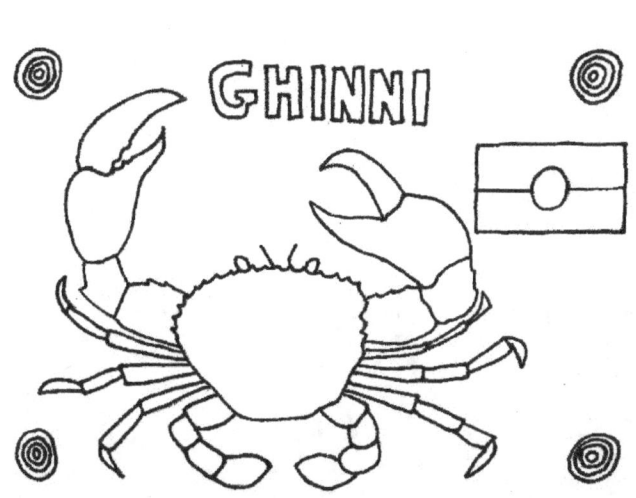

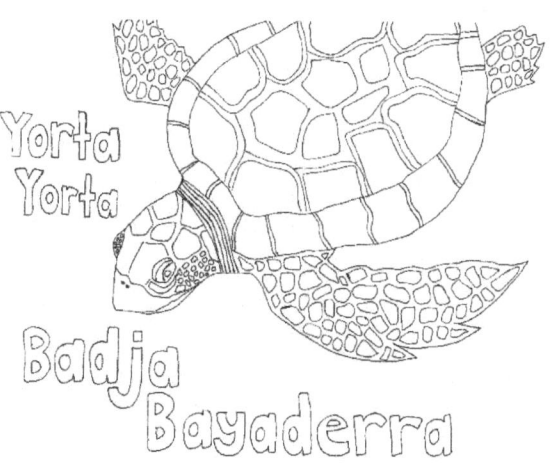

Copyright © 2017 Wanaruah Local Aboriginal Land Council

All rights reserved.

ISBN 13: 978-1973927082

ISBN 10: 197392708X

Published By Noel Downs Publishing

DEDICATION

This book is dedicated to Elders past and present, and to the youth who are our future.
Draw, paint, sing, dance and play at every opportunity

ACKNOWLEDGMENTS

I would like to acknowledge the traditional custodians of the land I am on, their spirits for speaking to me, making me feel at home and keeping our community strong.

Introduction

NAIDOC stands for National Aborigines and Islanders Day Observance Committee. Its origins can be traced to the emergence of Aboriginal groups in the 1920's which sought to increase awareness in the wider community of the status and treatment of Indigenous Australians.

NAIDOC Week is held in the first full week of July. It is a time to celebrate Aboriginal and Torres Strait Islander history, culture and achievements and is an opportunity to recognise the contributions that Indigenous Australians make to our country and our society.

NAIDOC is celebrated not only in Indigenous communities but by Australians from all walks of life. The week is a great opportunity to participate in a range of activities and to support your local Aboriginal and Torres Strait Islander community.

We encourage all Australians to participate in the celebrations and activities that take place across the nation during NAIDOC Week.

This book has been developed by the Wanaruah Local Aboriginal Land Council Community as a celebration of local artists young and not as young and to share their art. Contributions were requested from the Aboriginal community and staff of the Wanaruah LALC.

The list of contributing artists is at the back of the book.

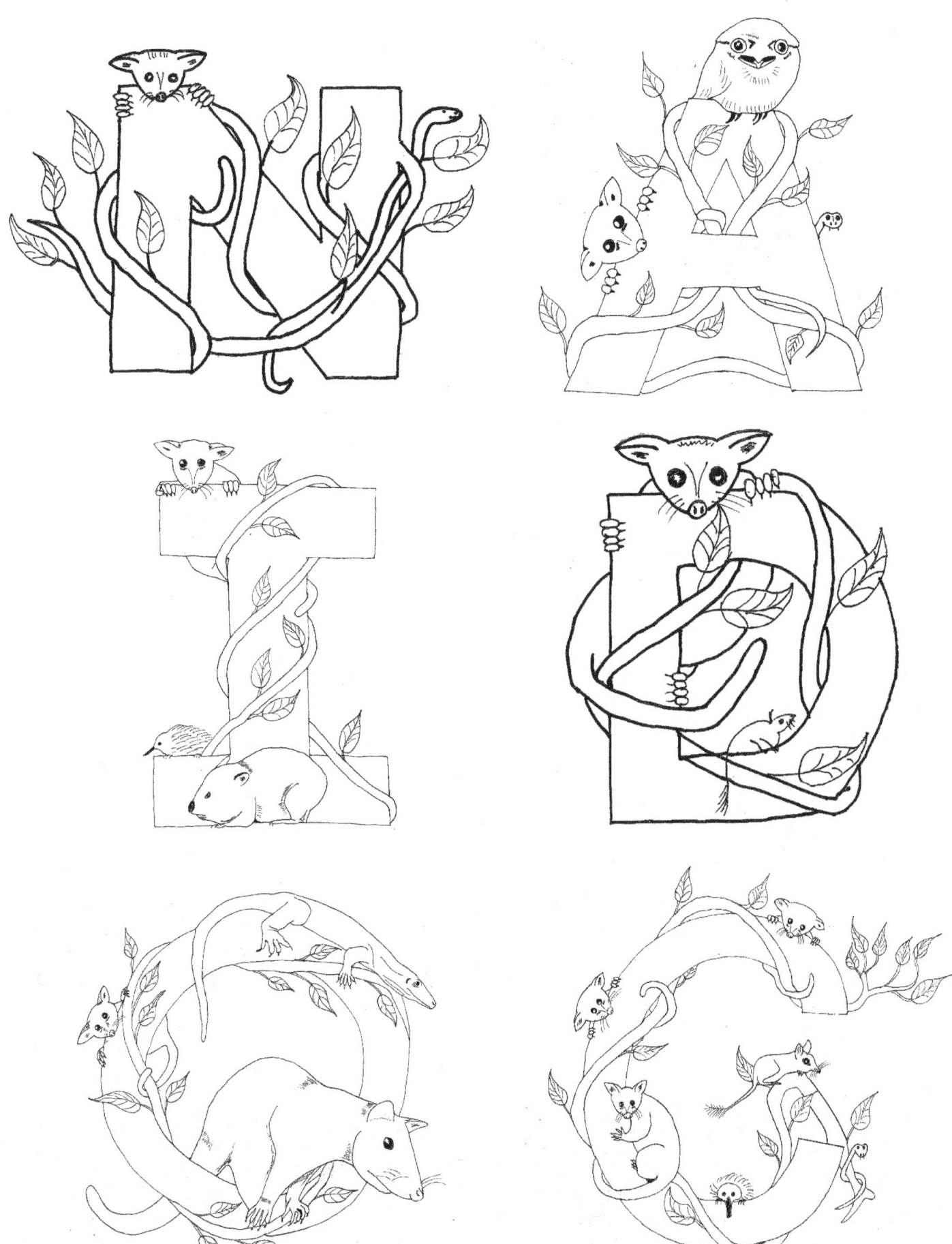

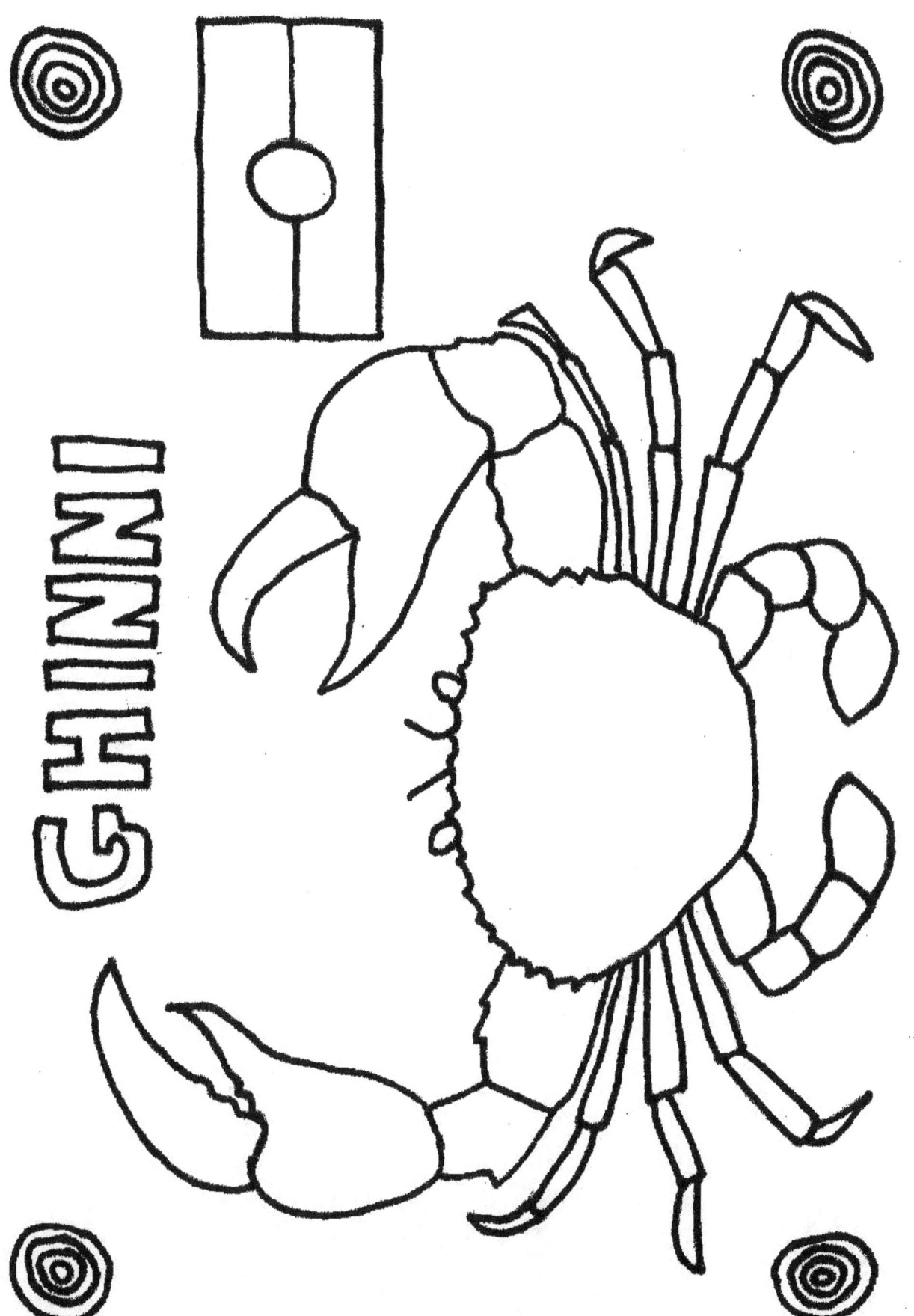

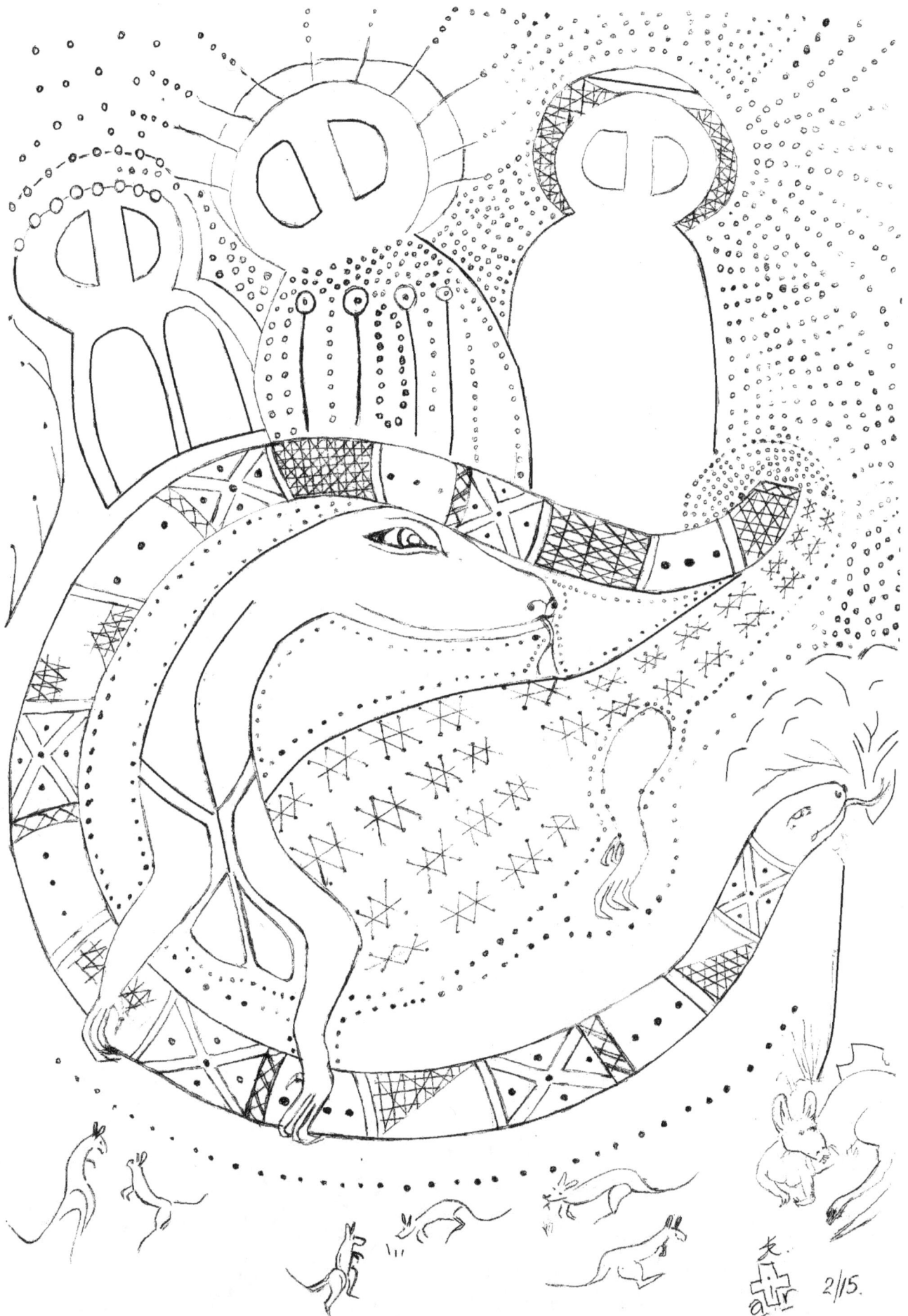

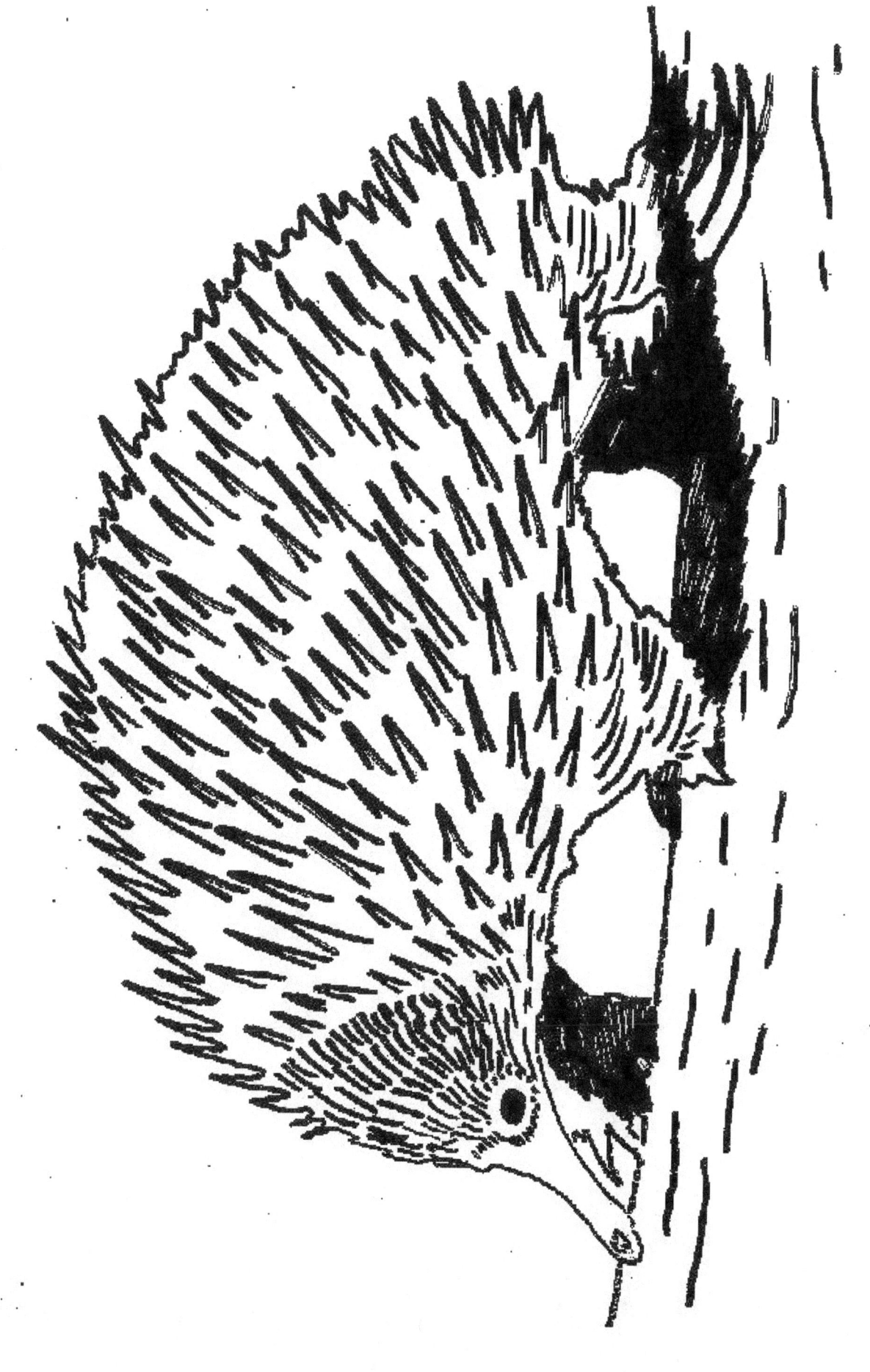

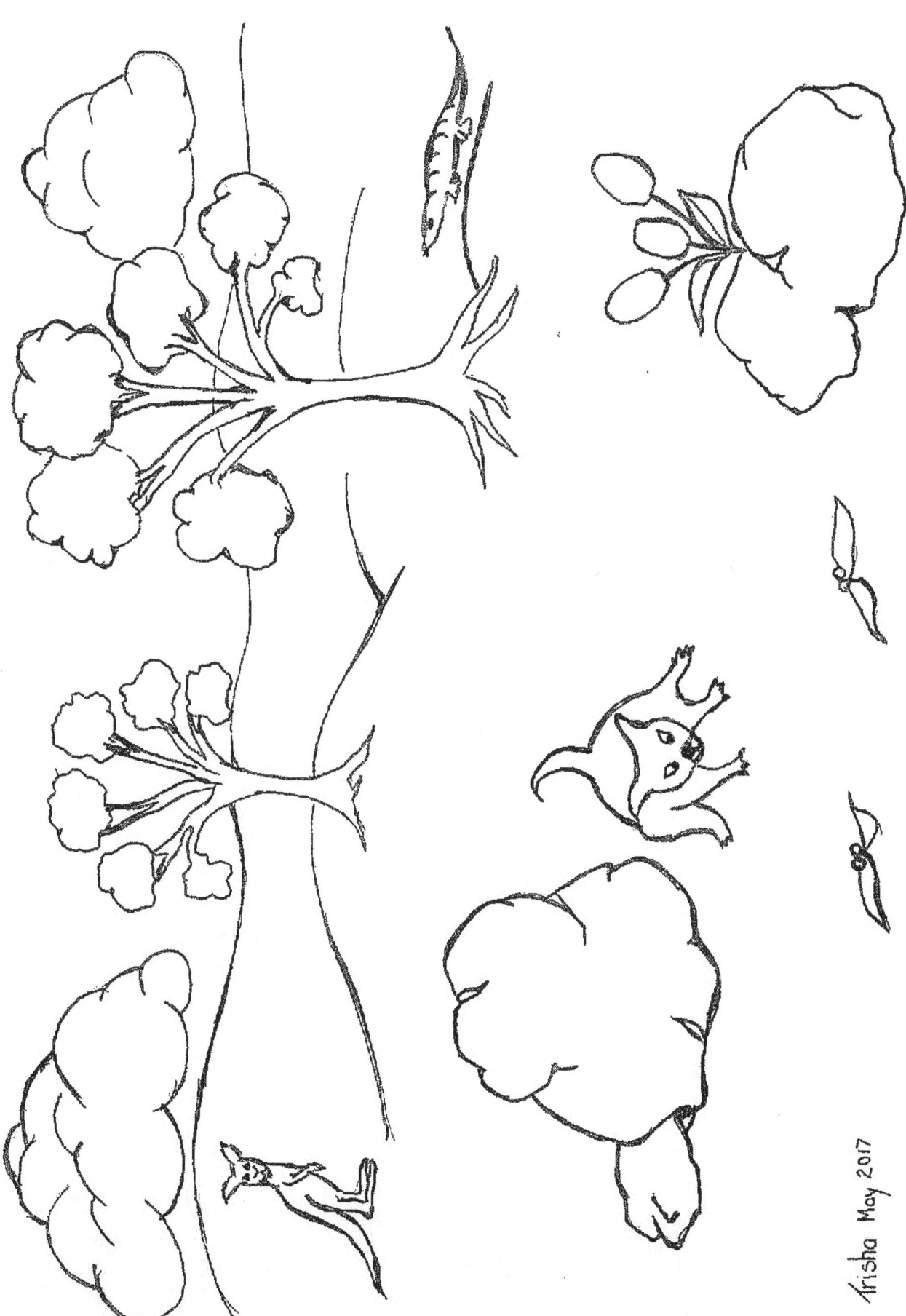

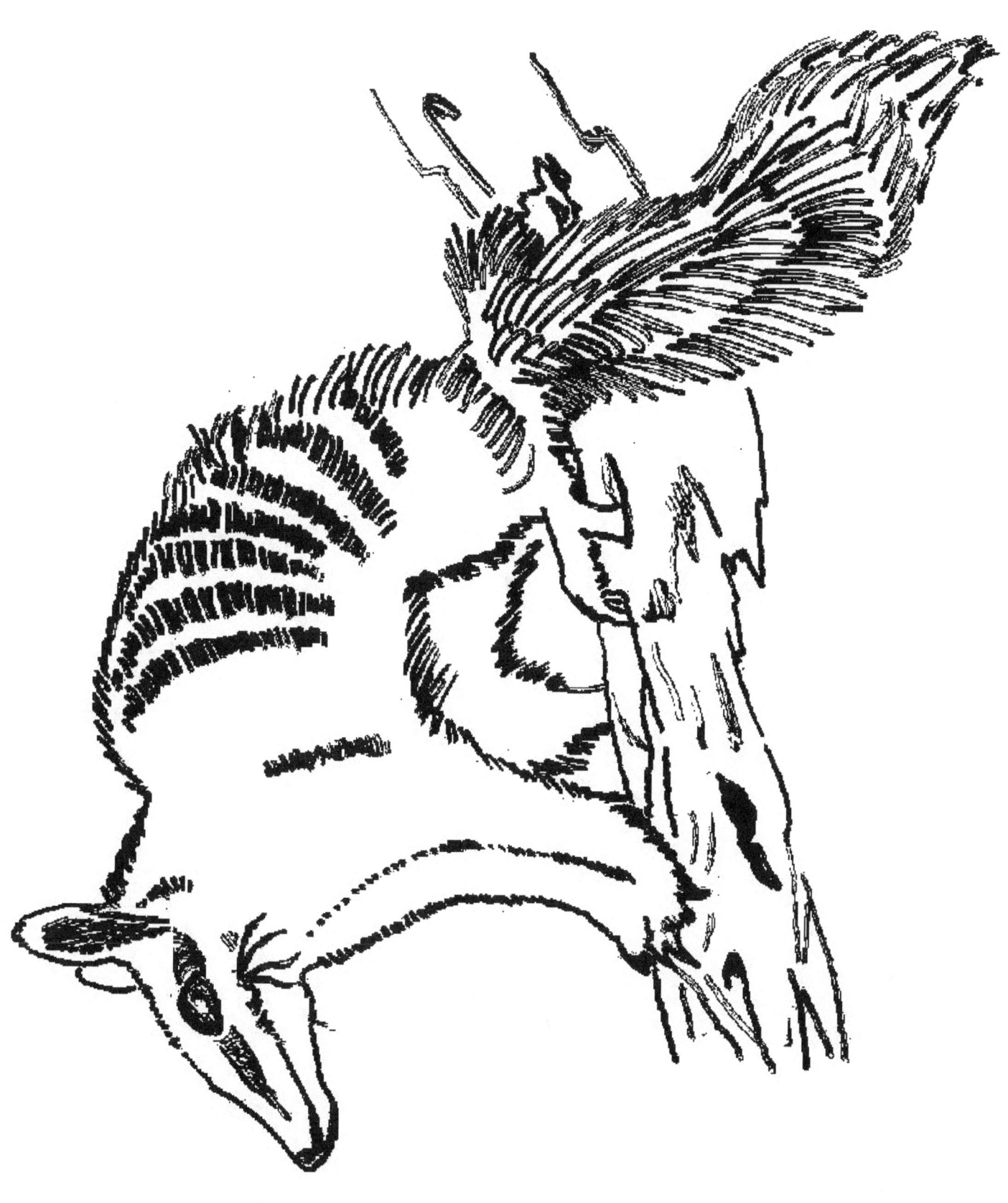

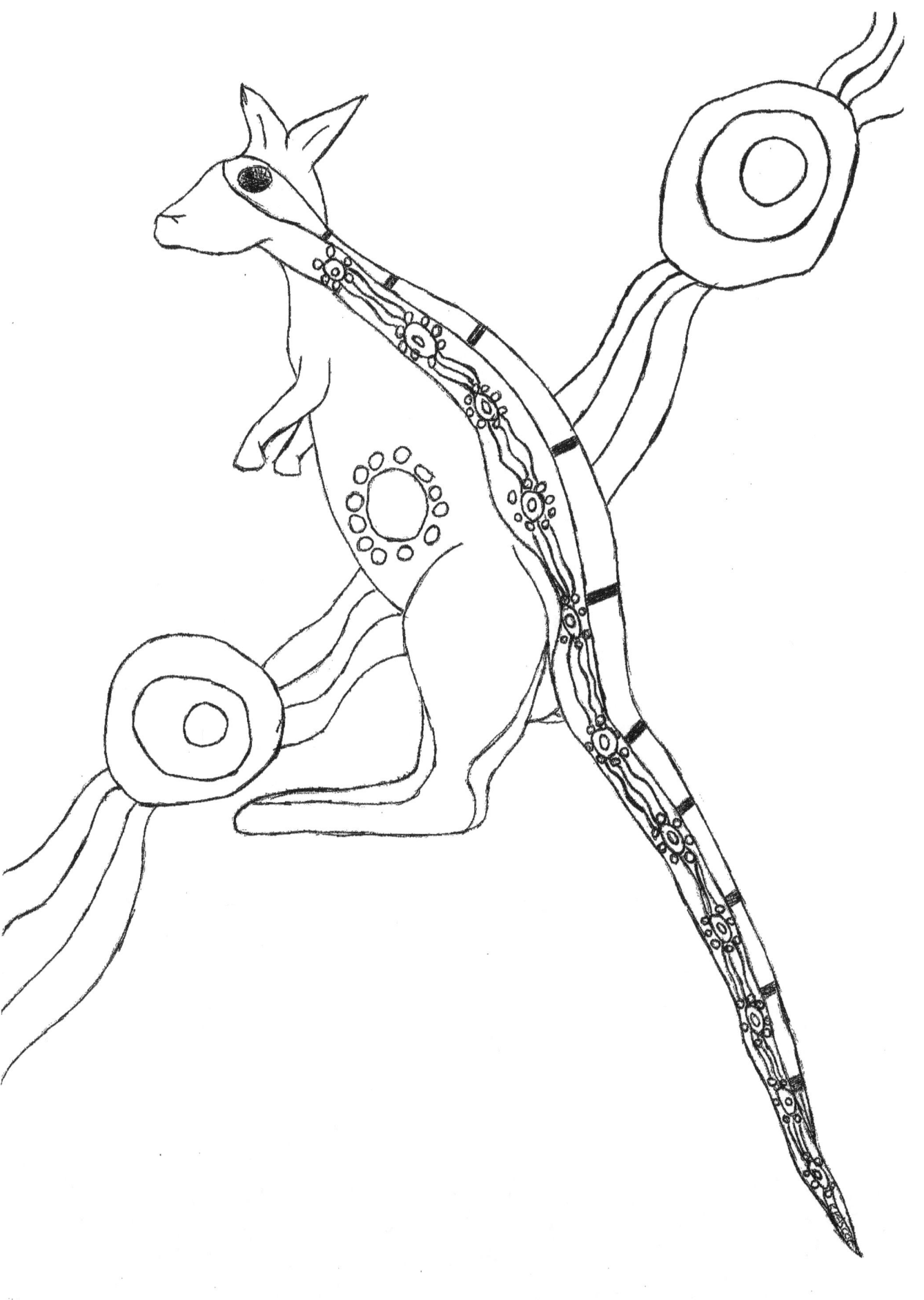

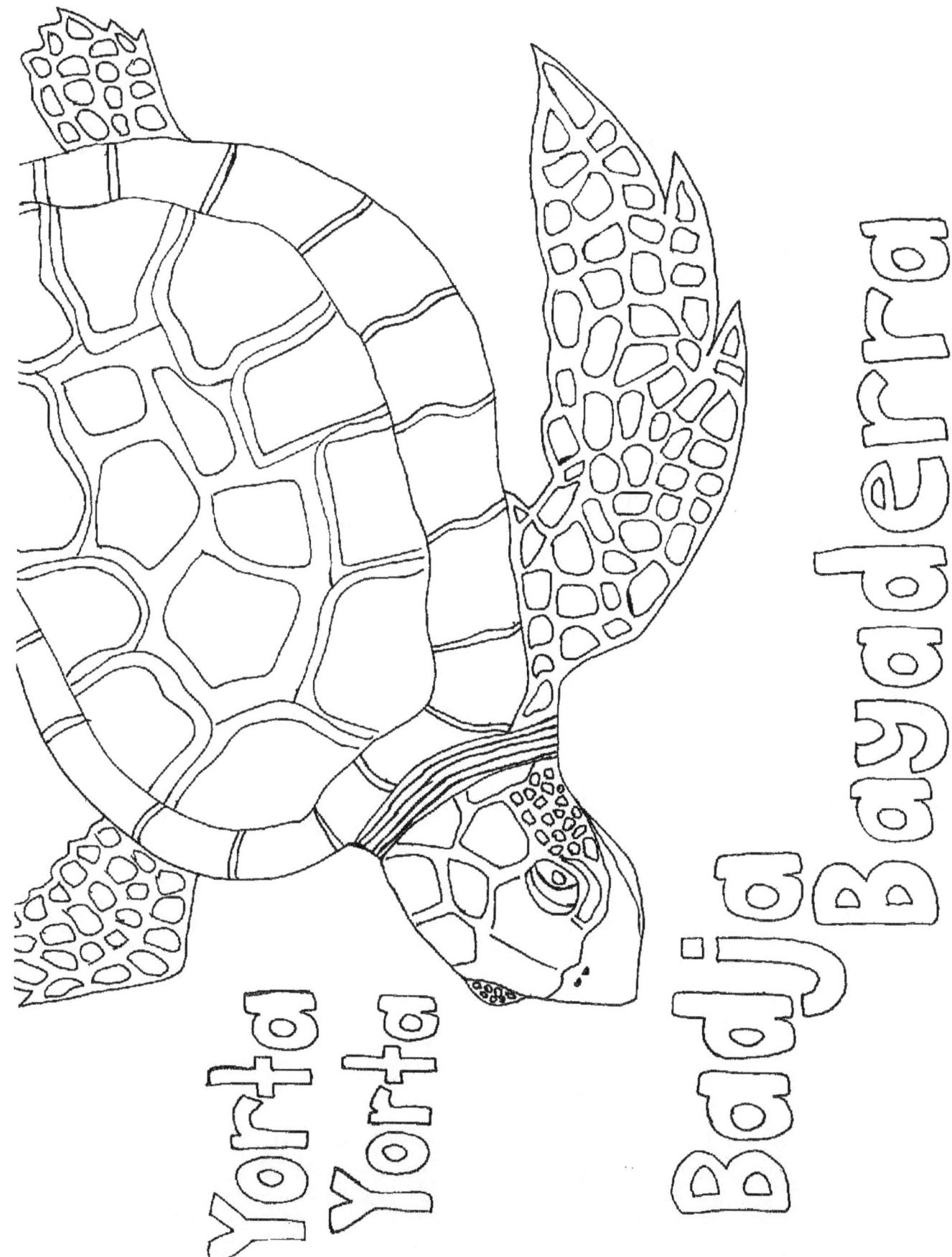

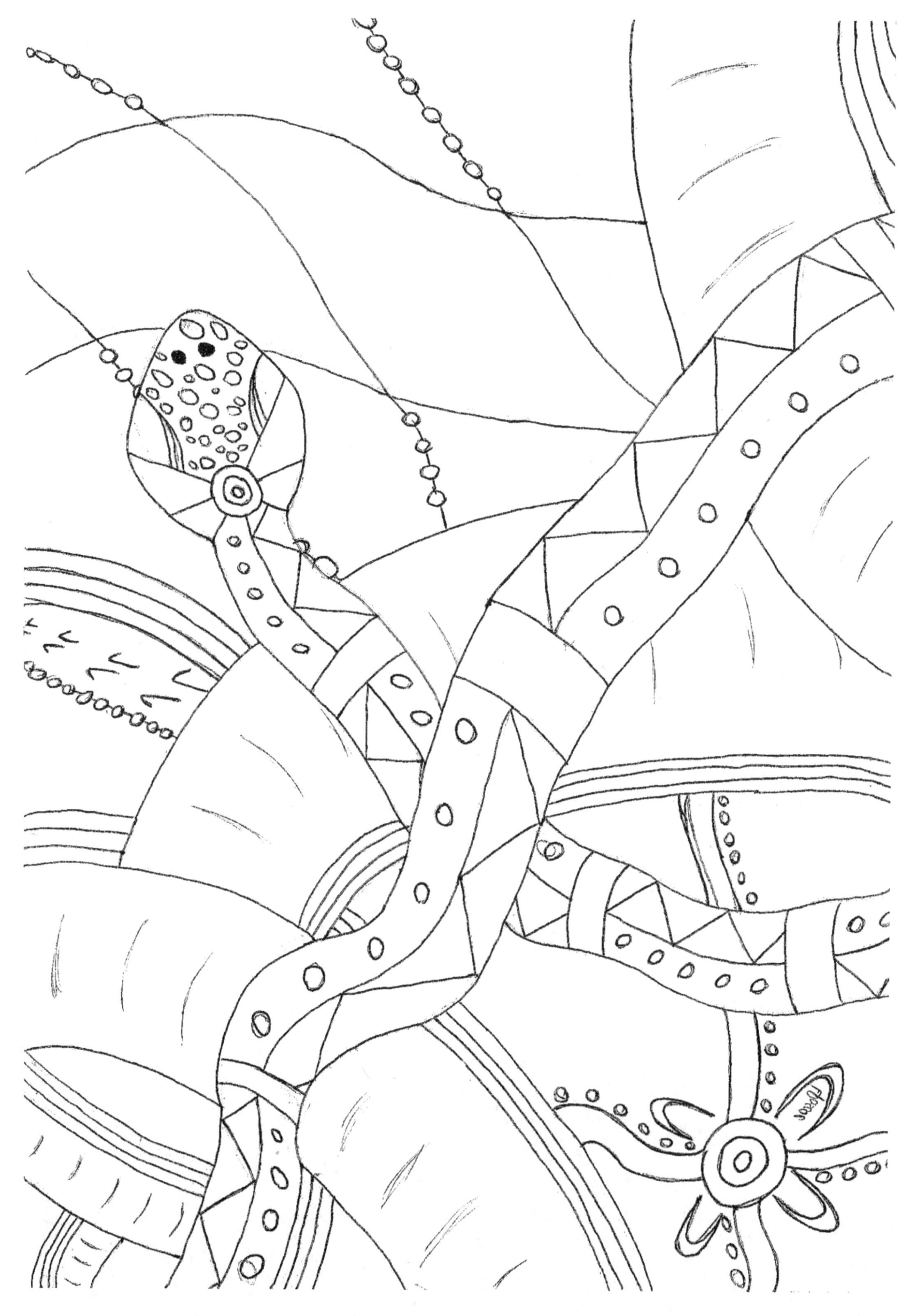

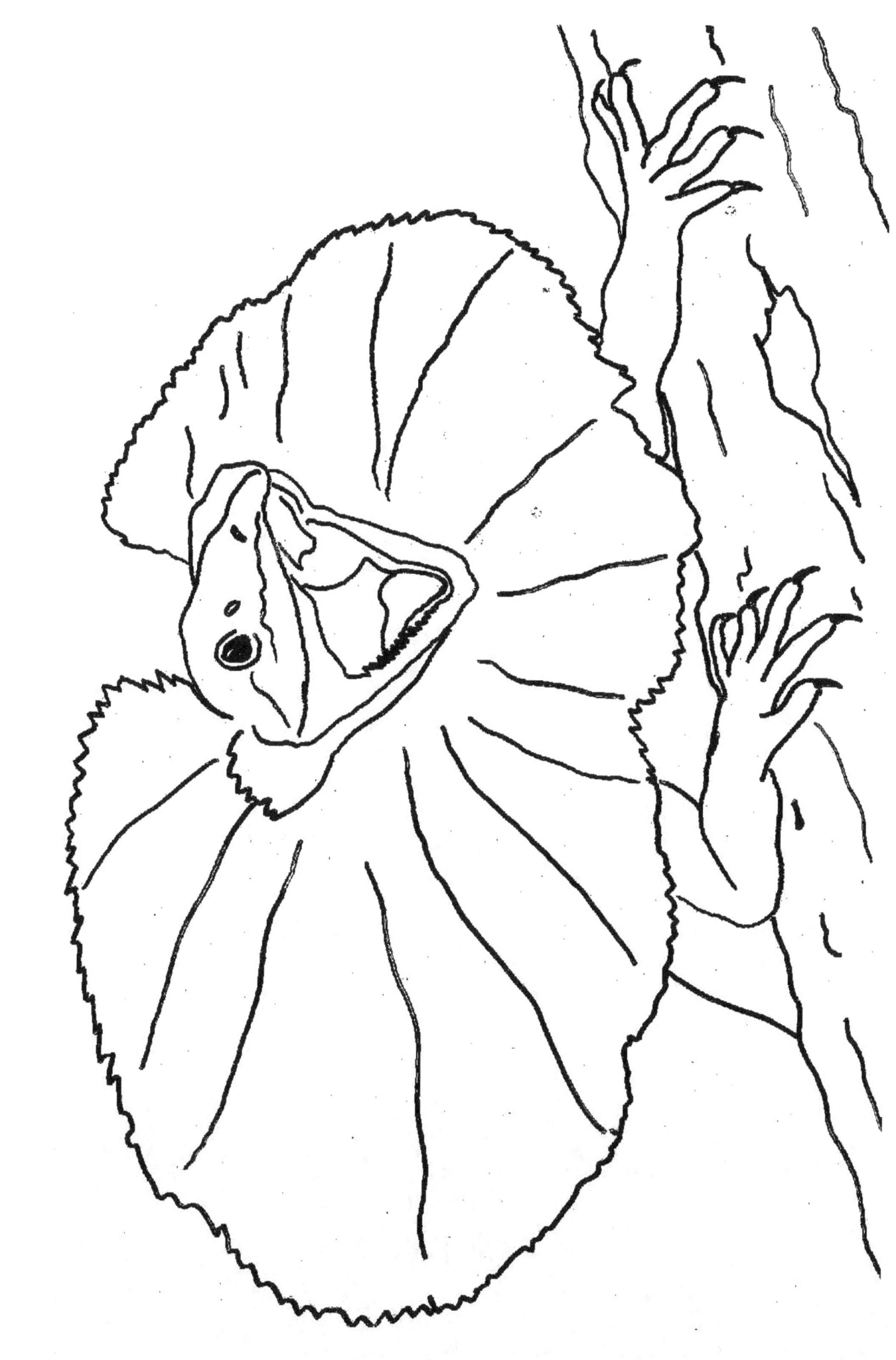

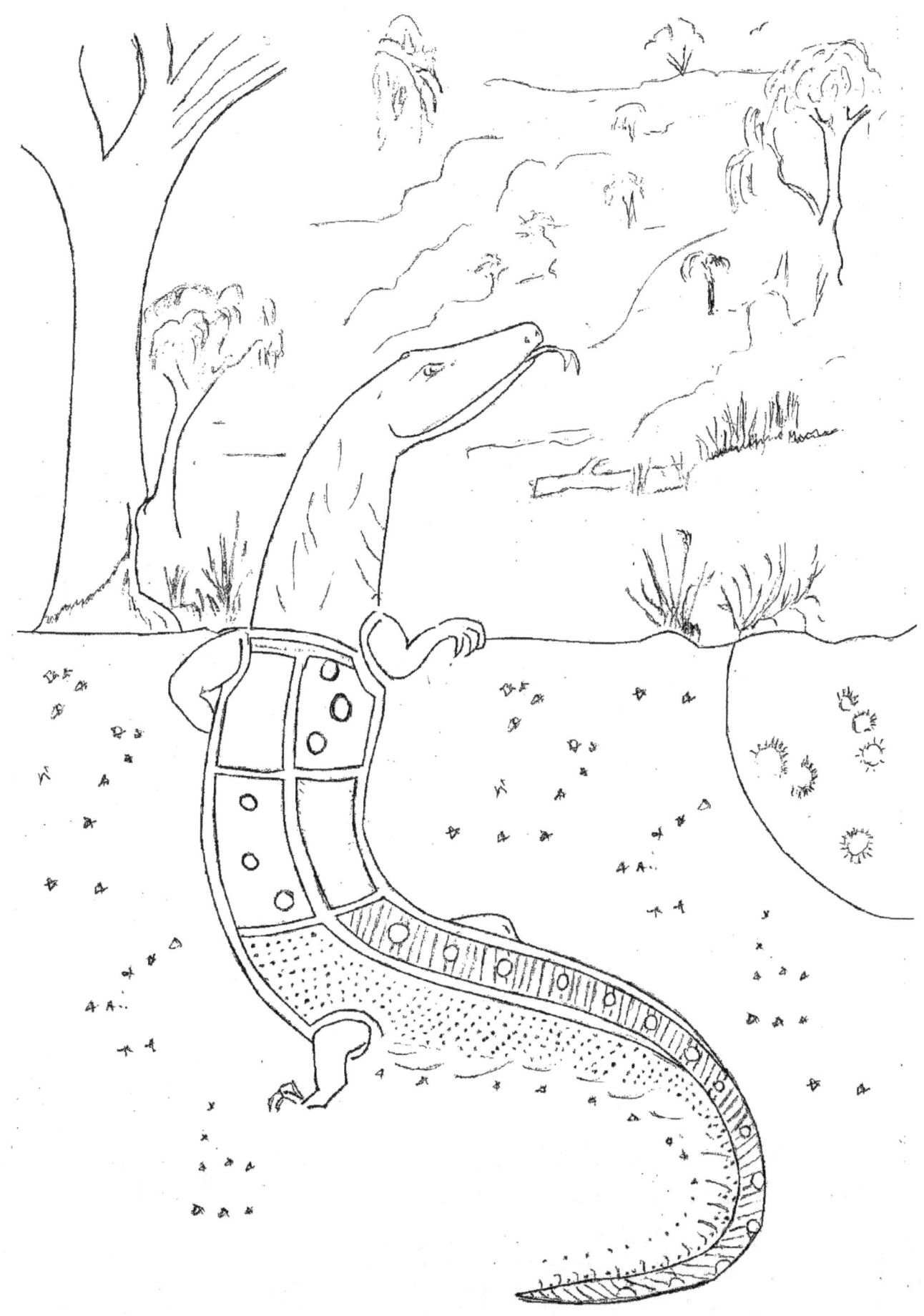

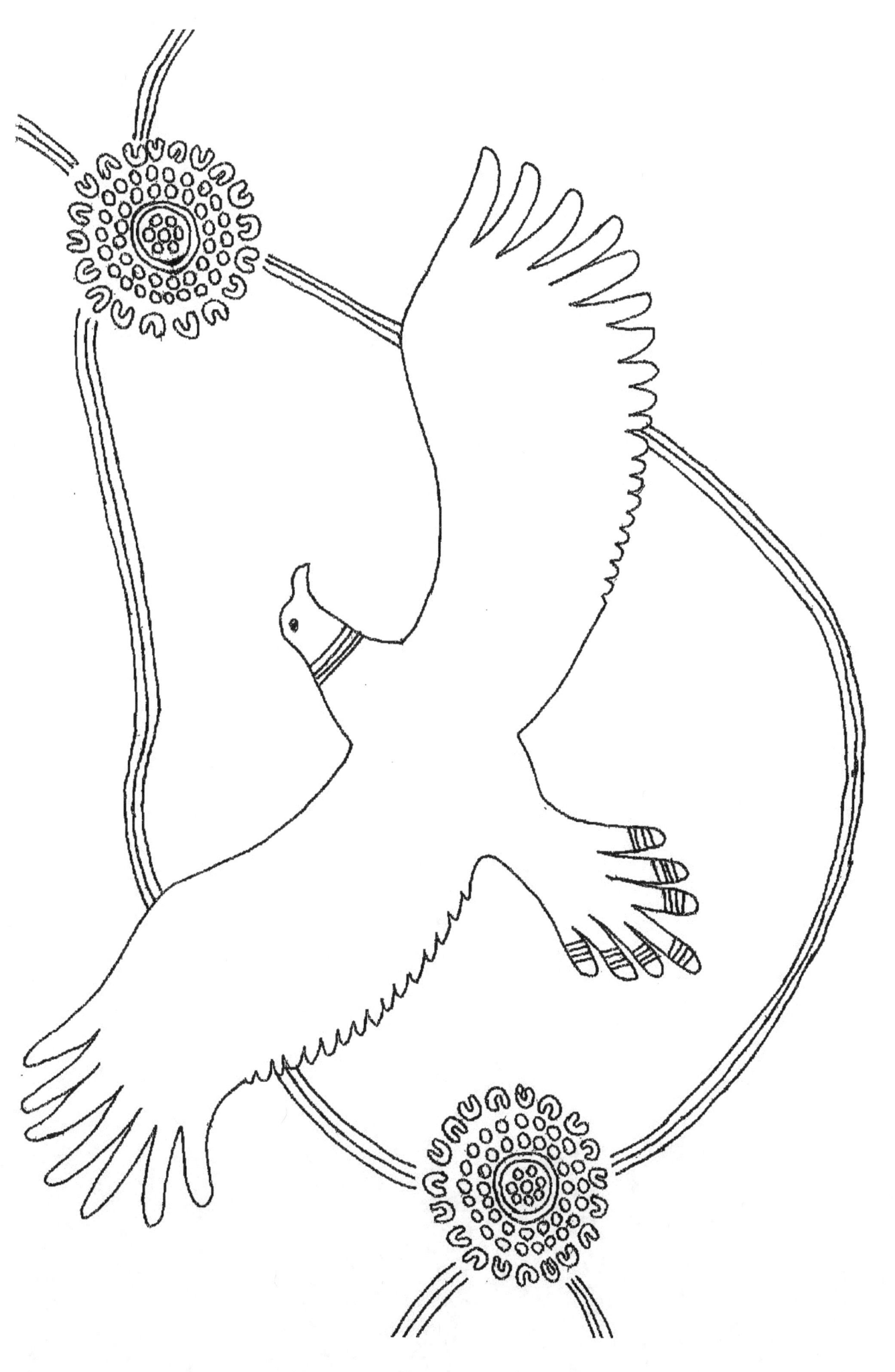

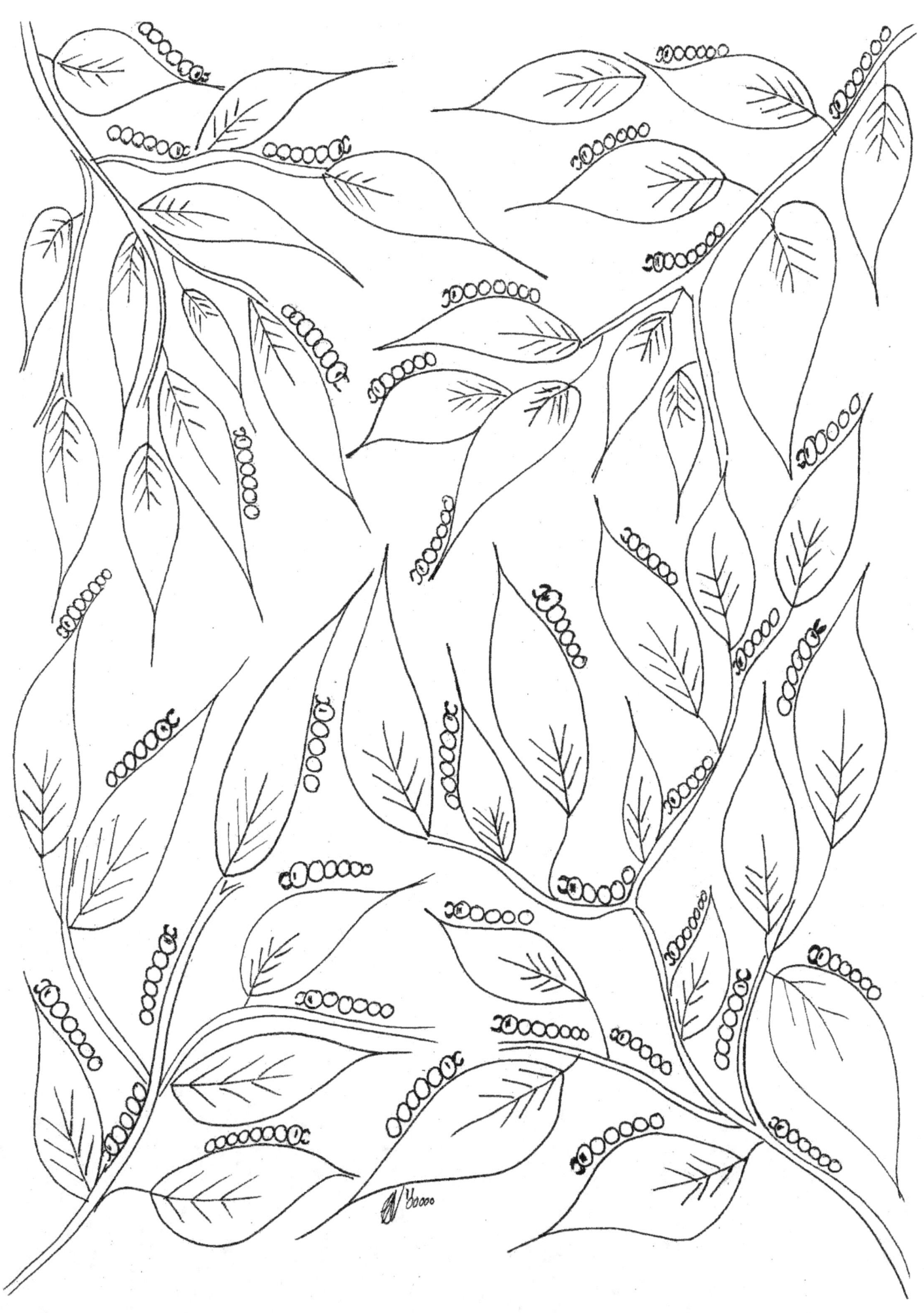

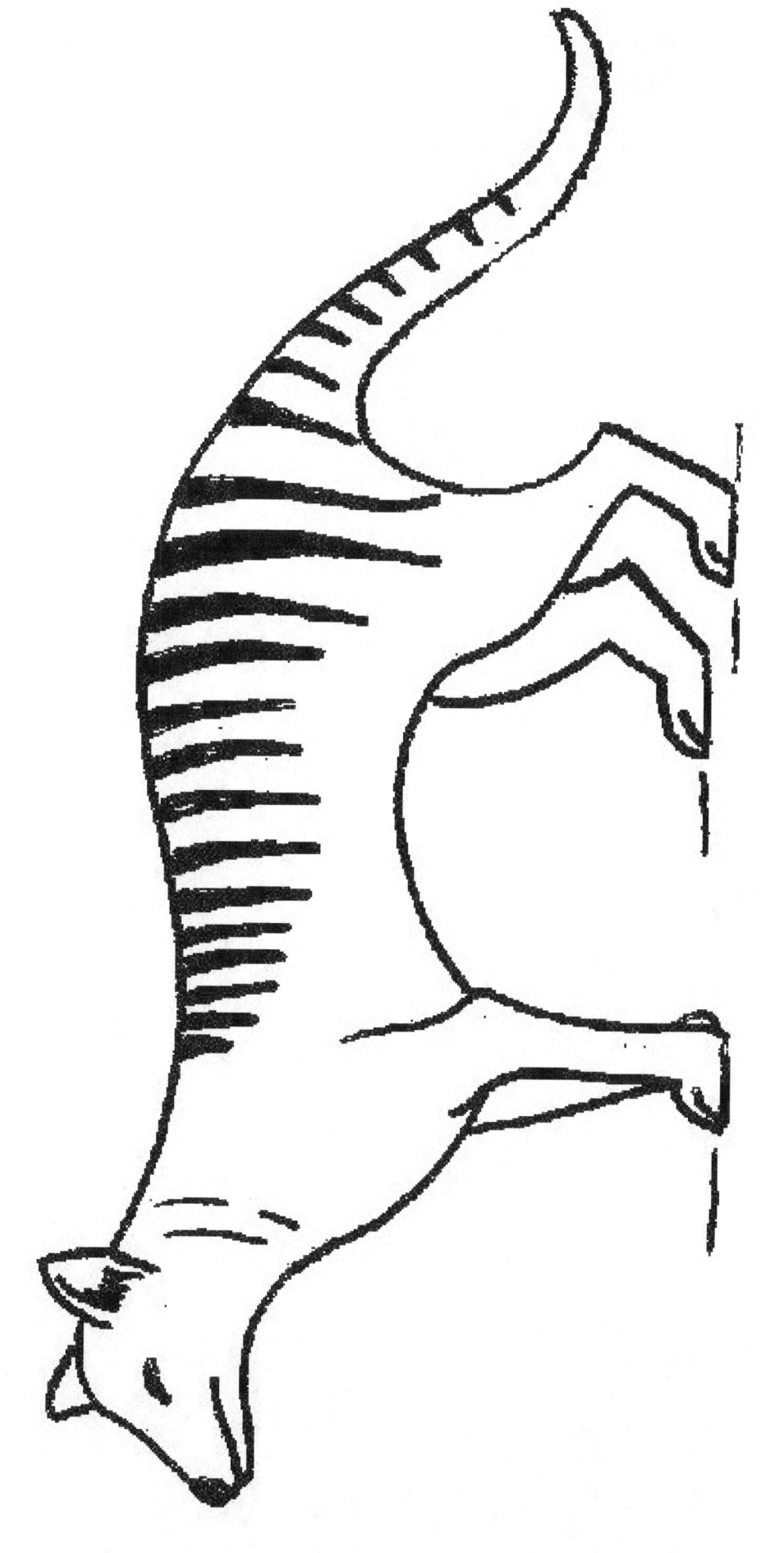

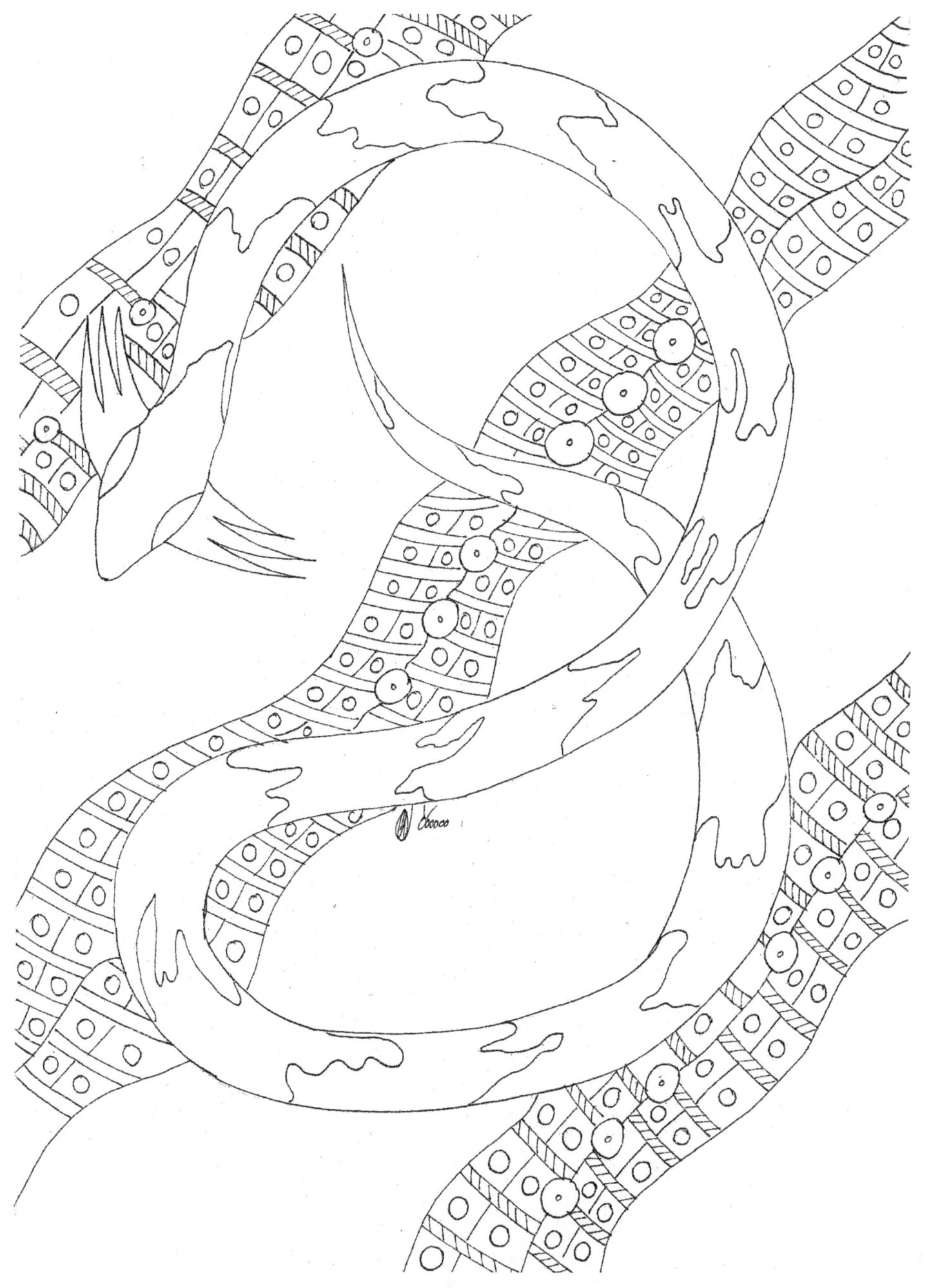

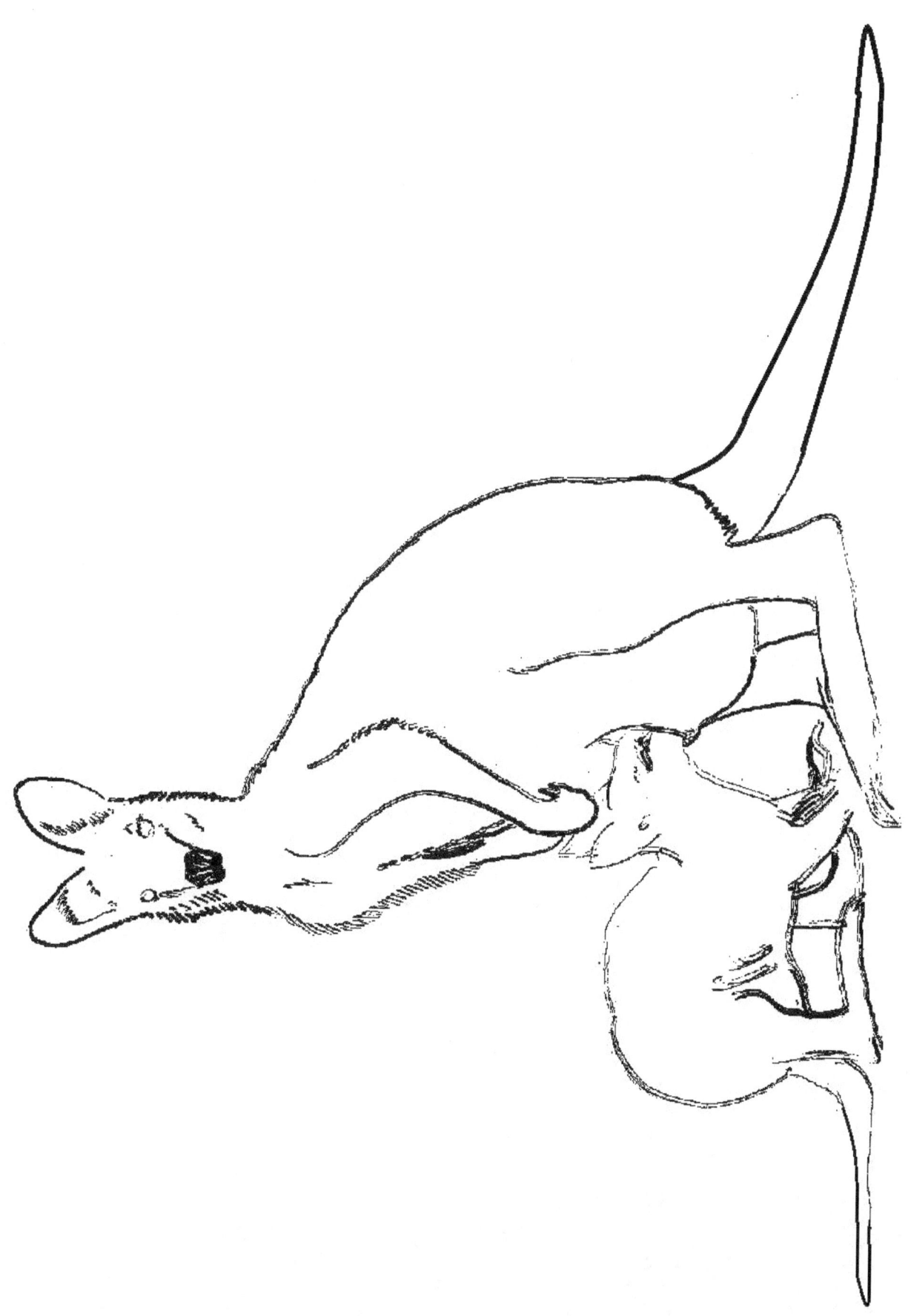

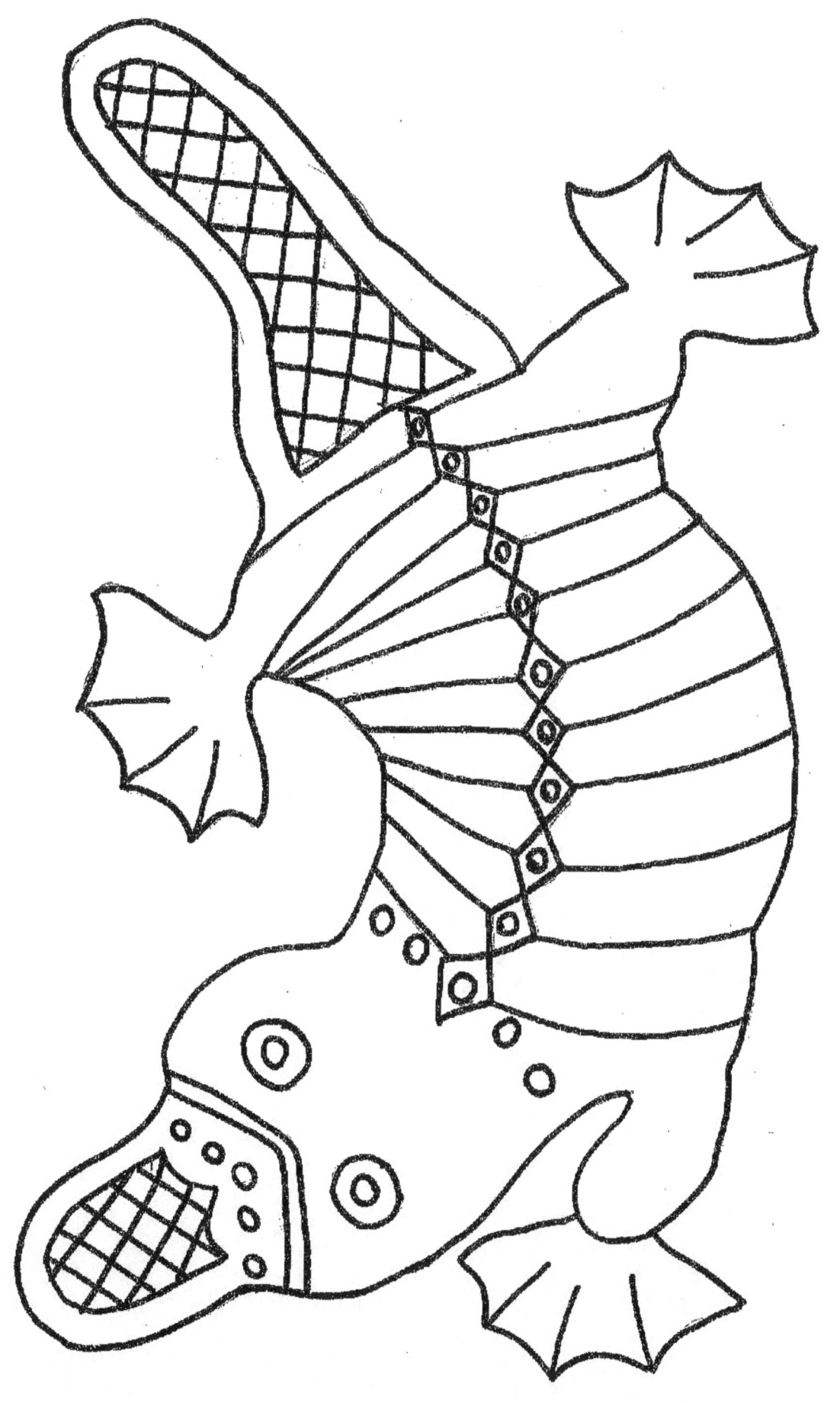

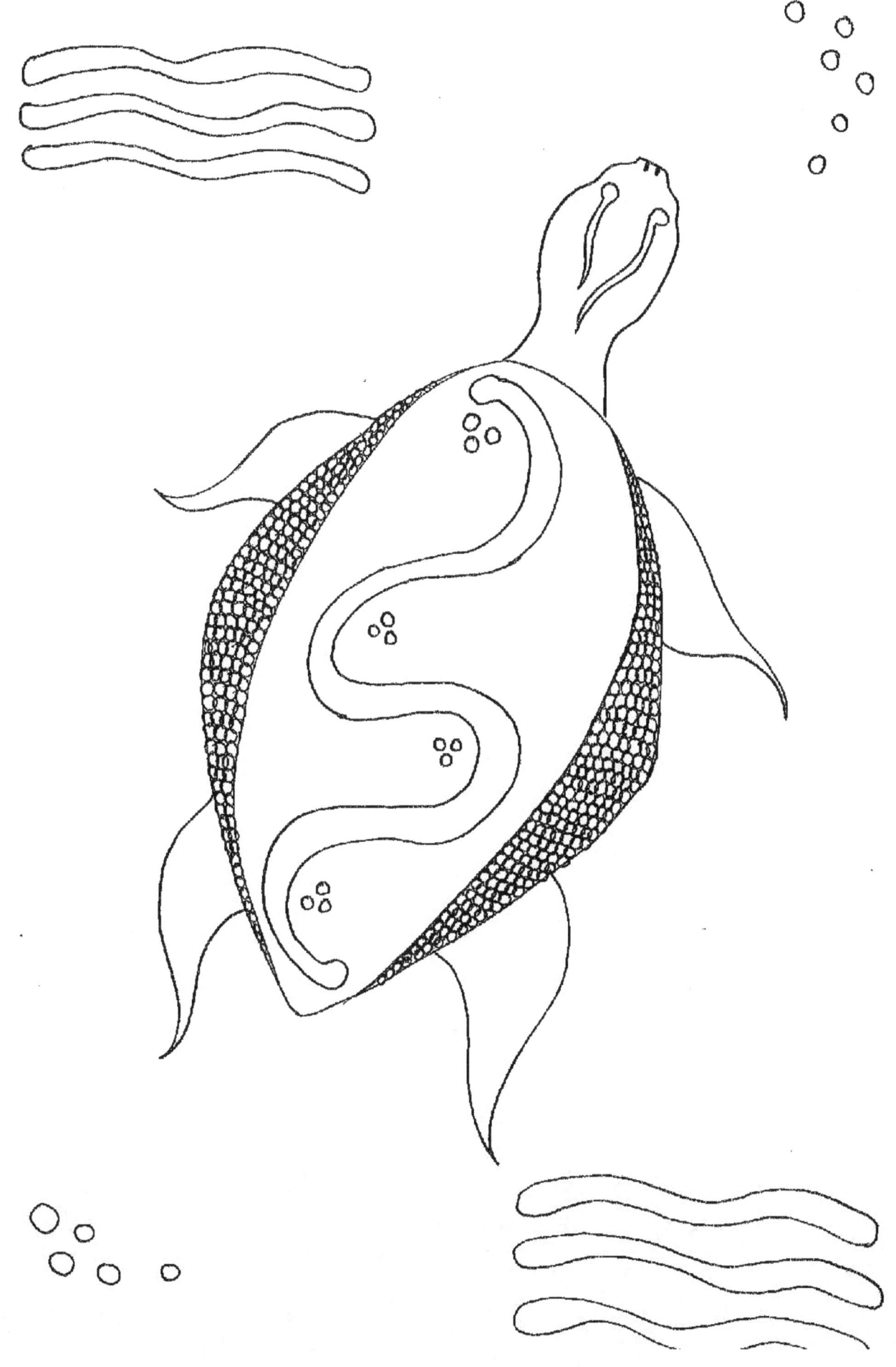

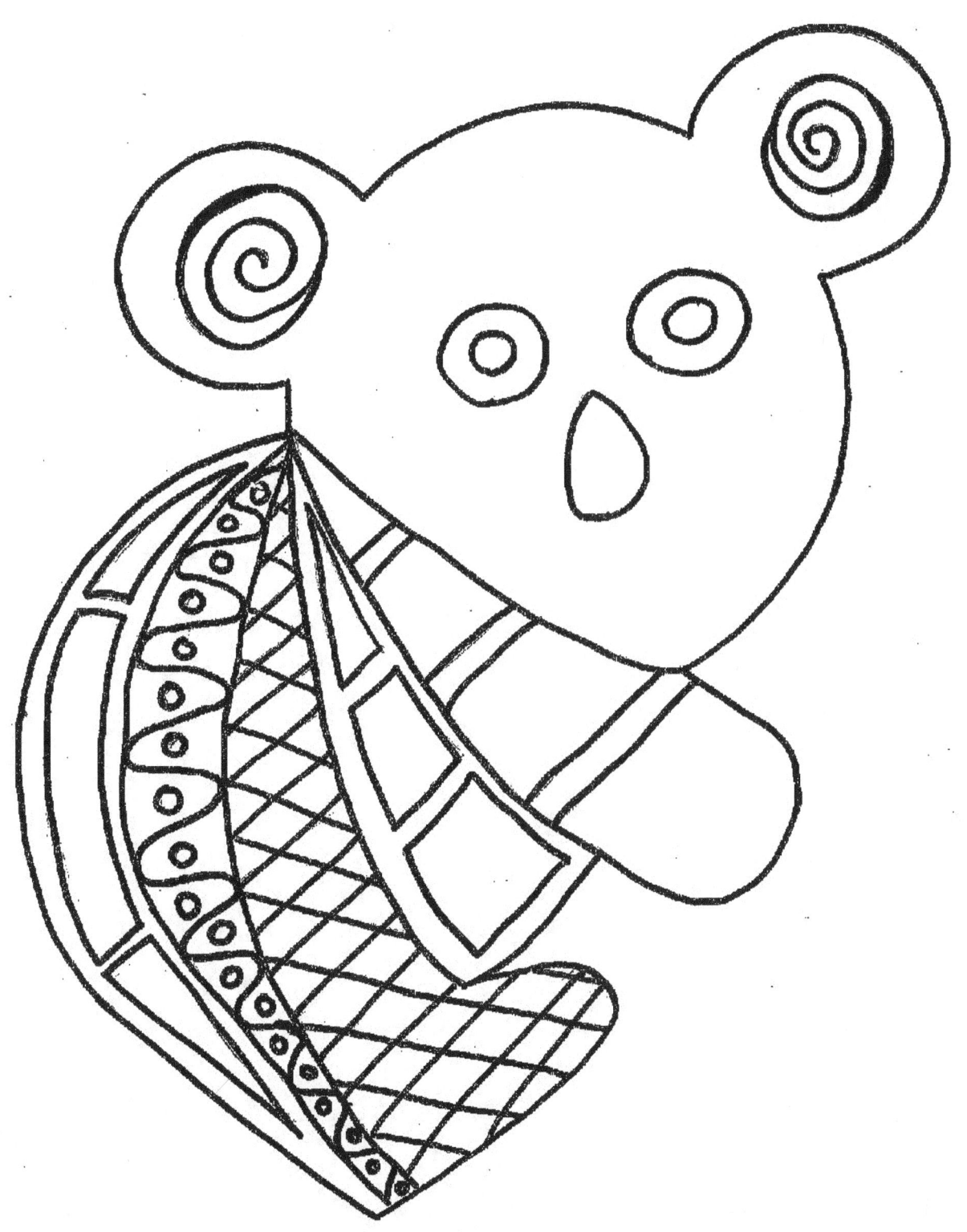

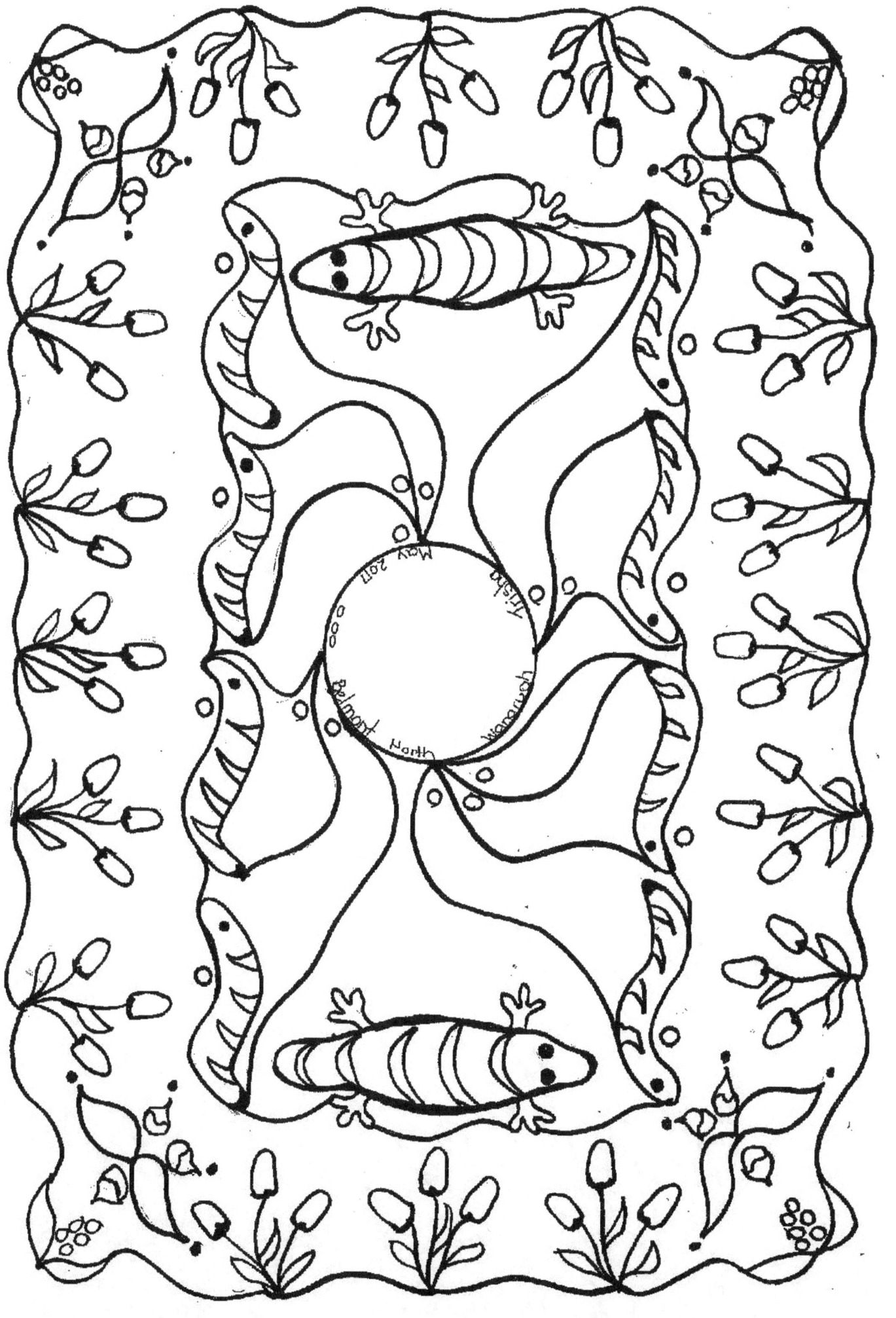

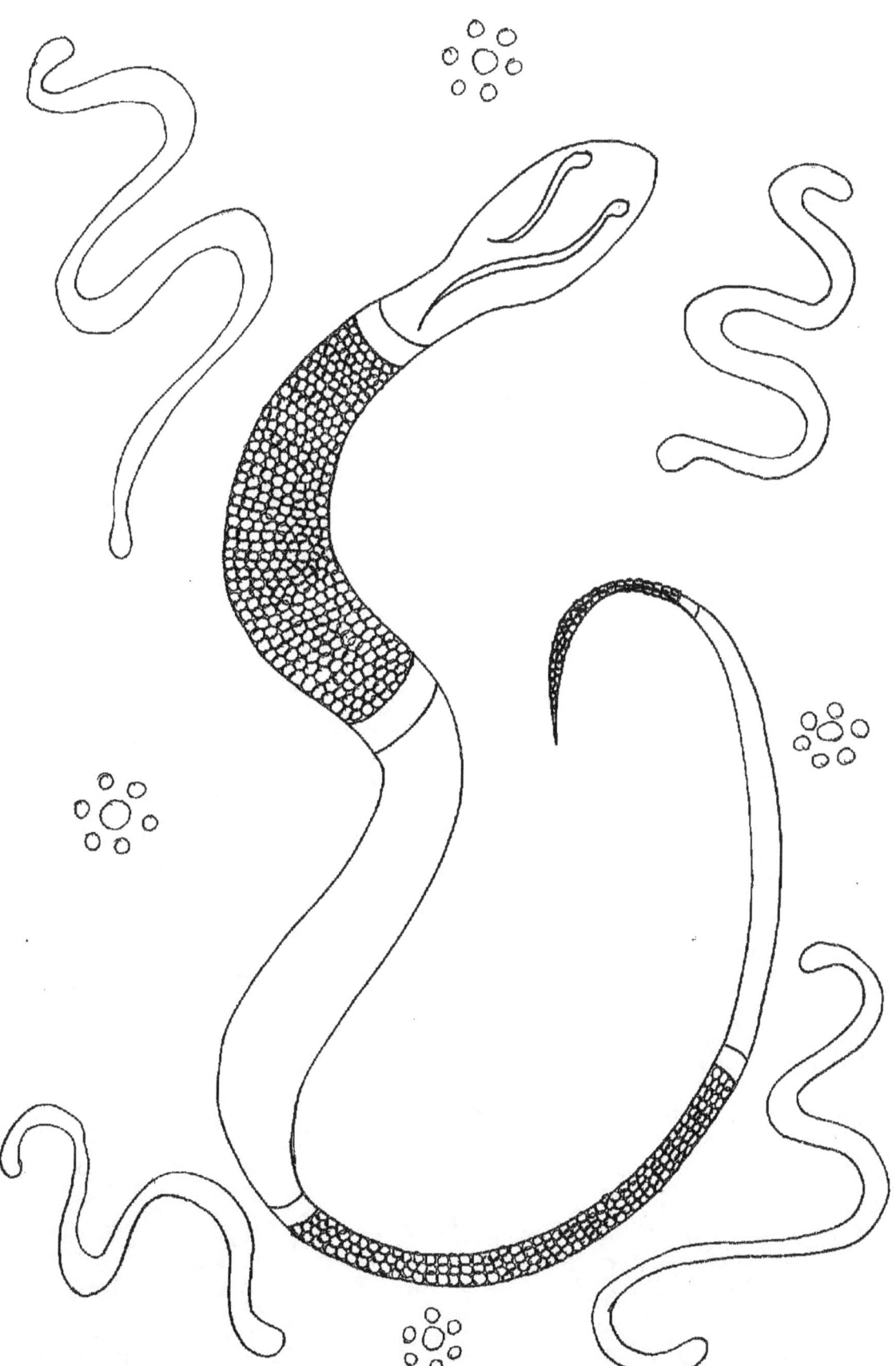

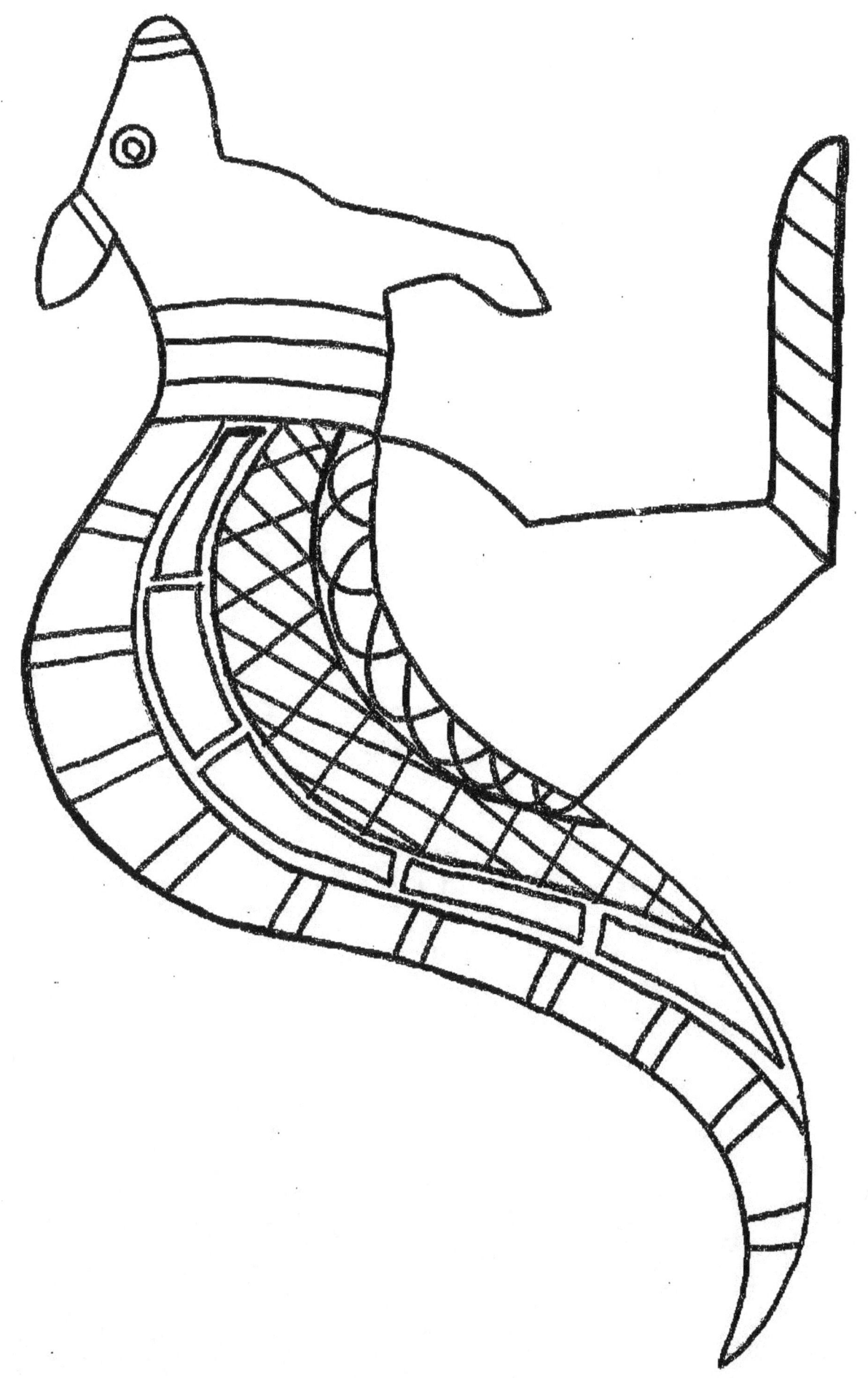

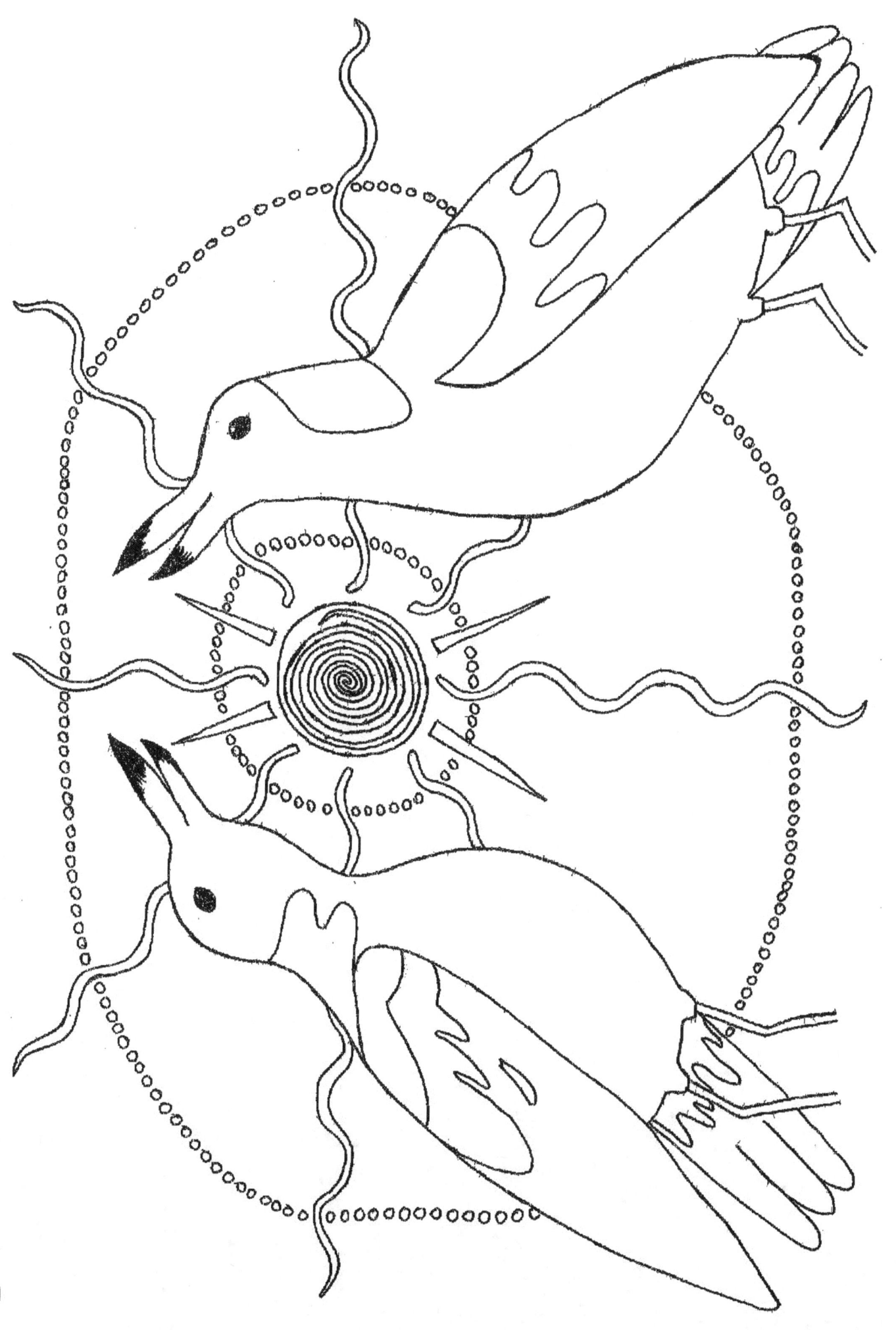

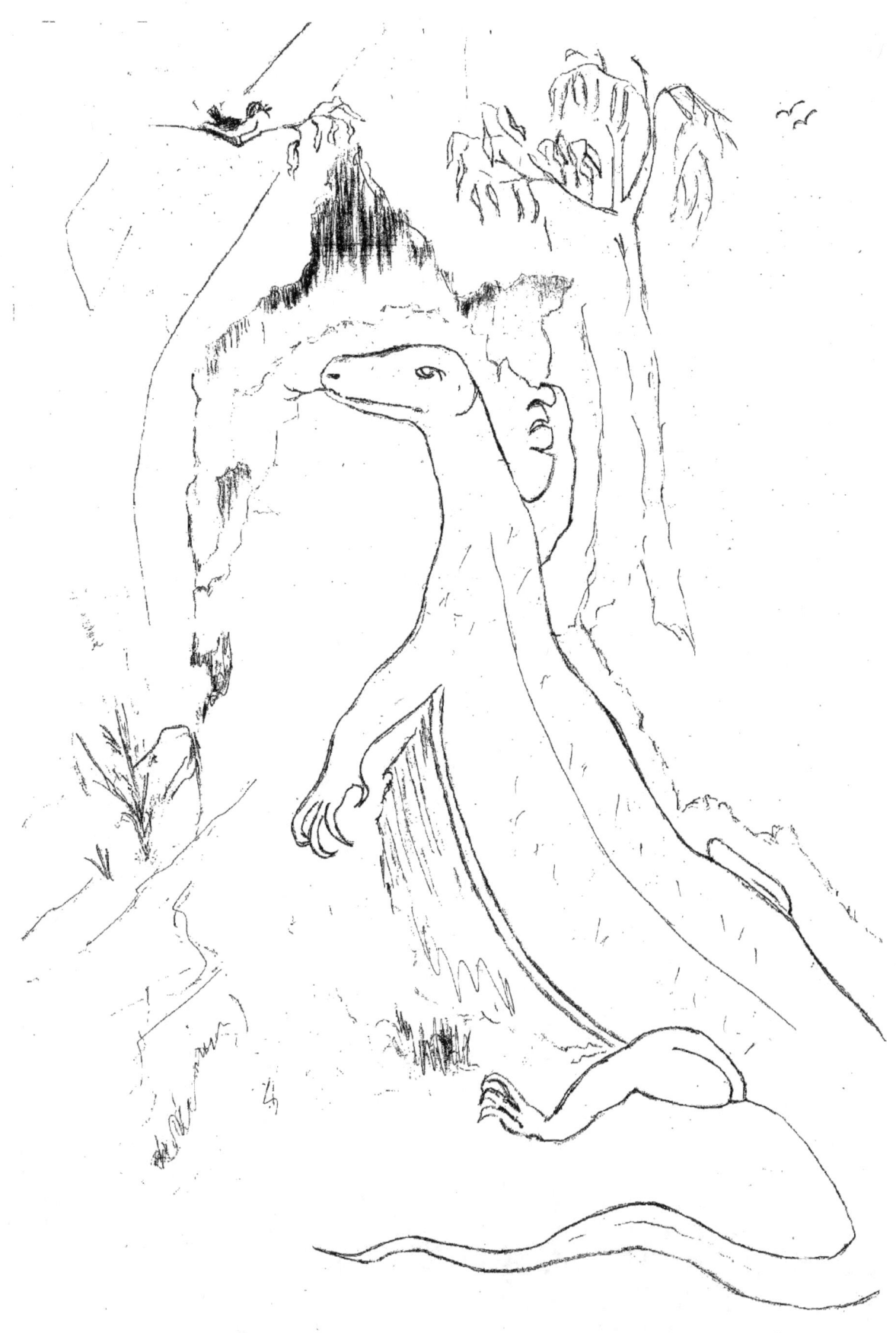

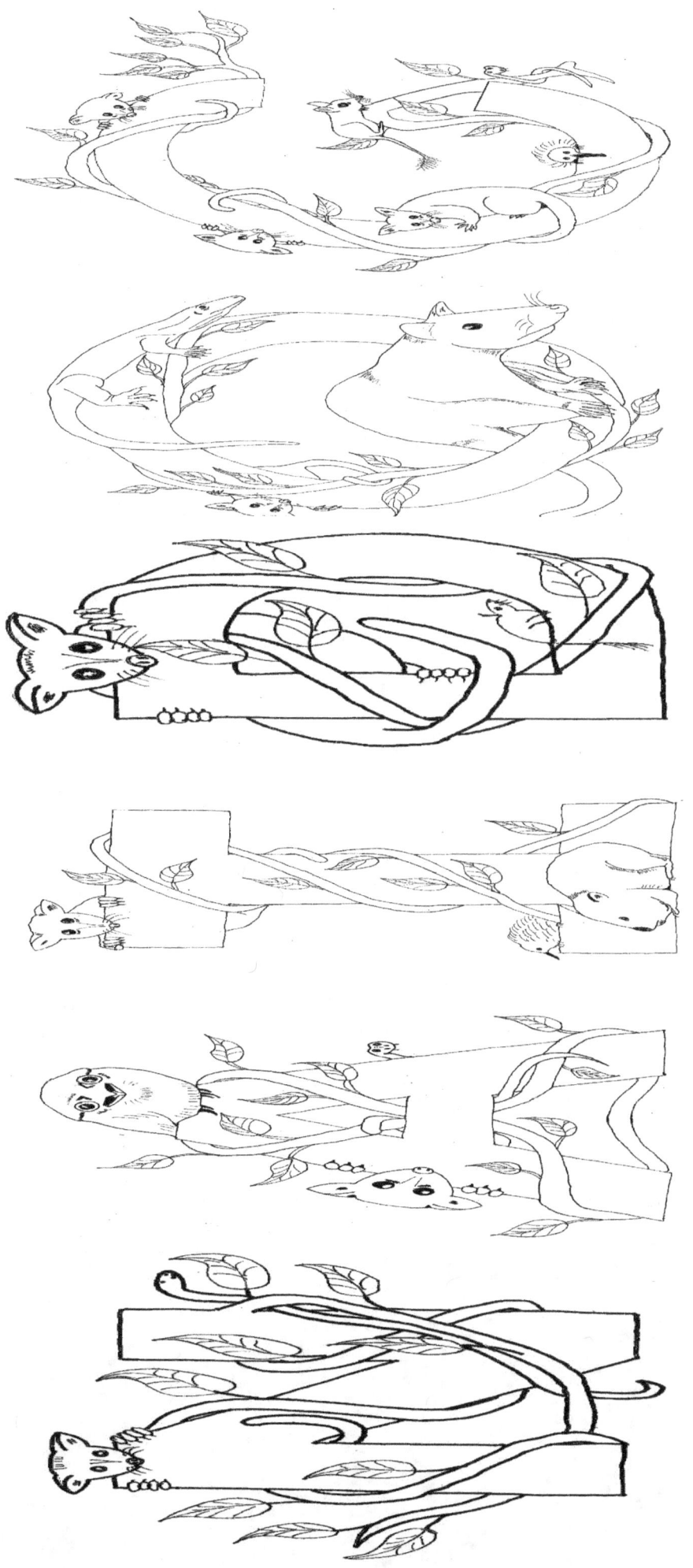

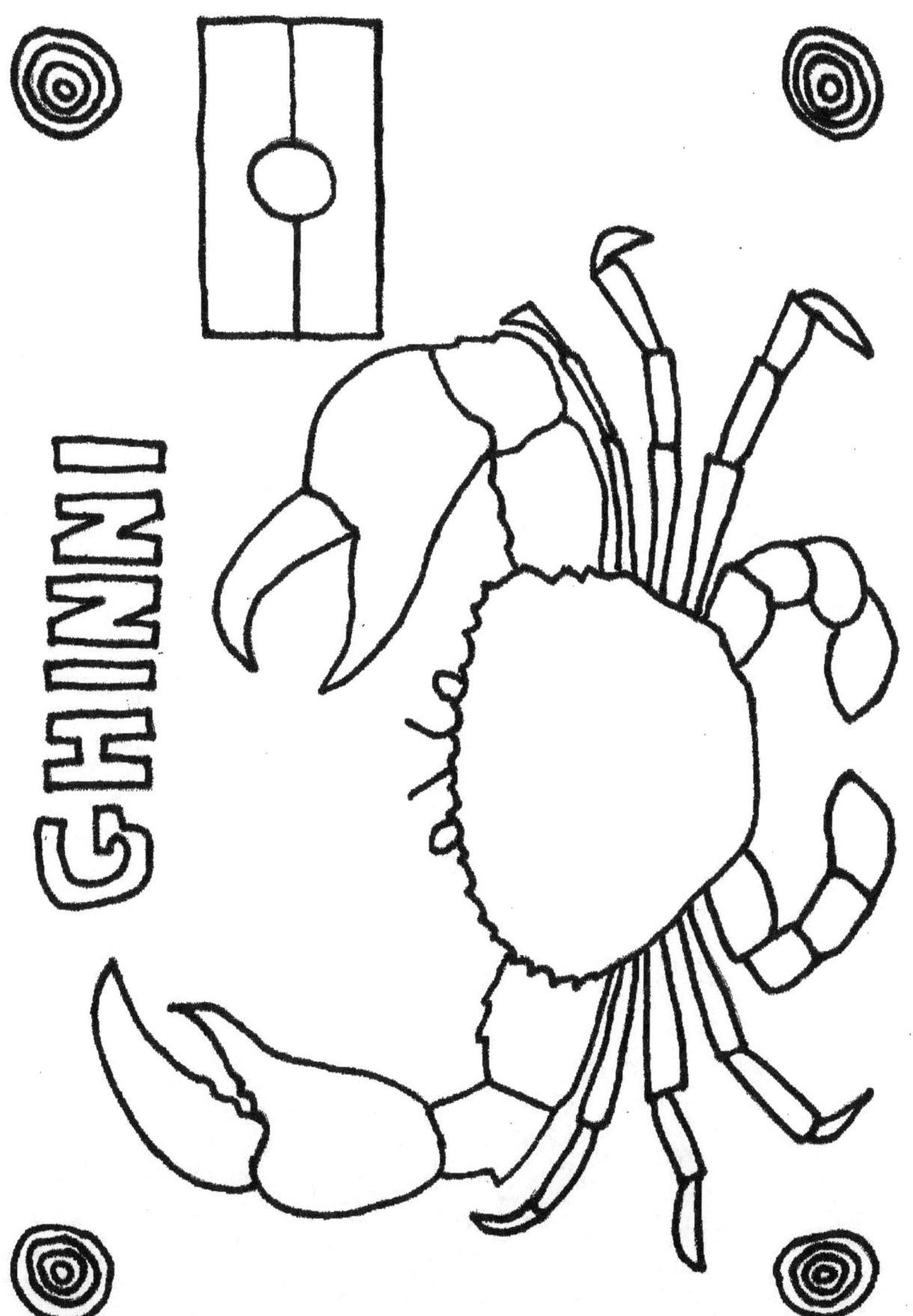

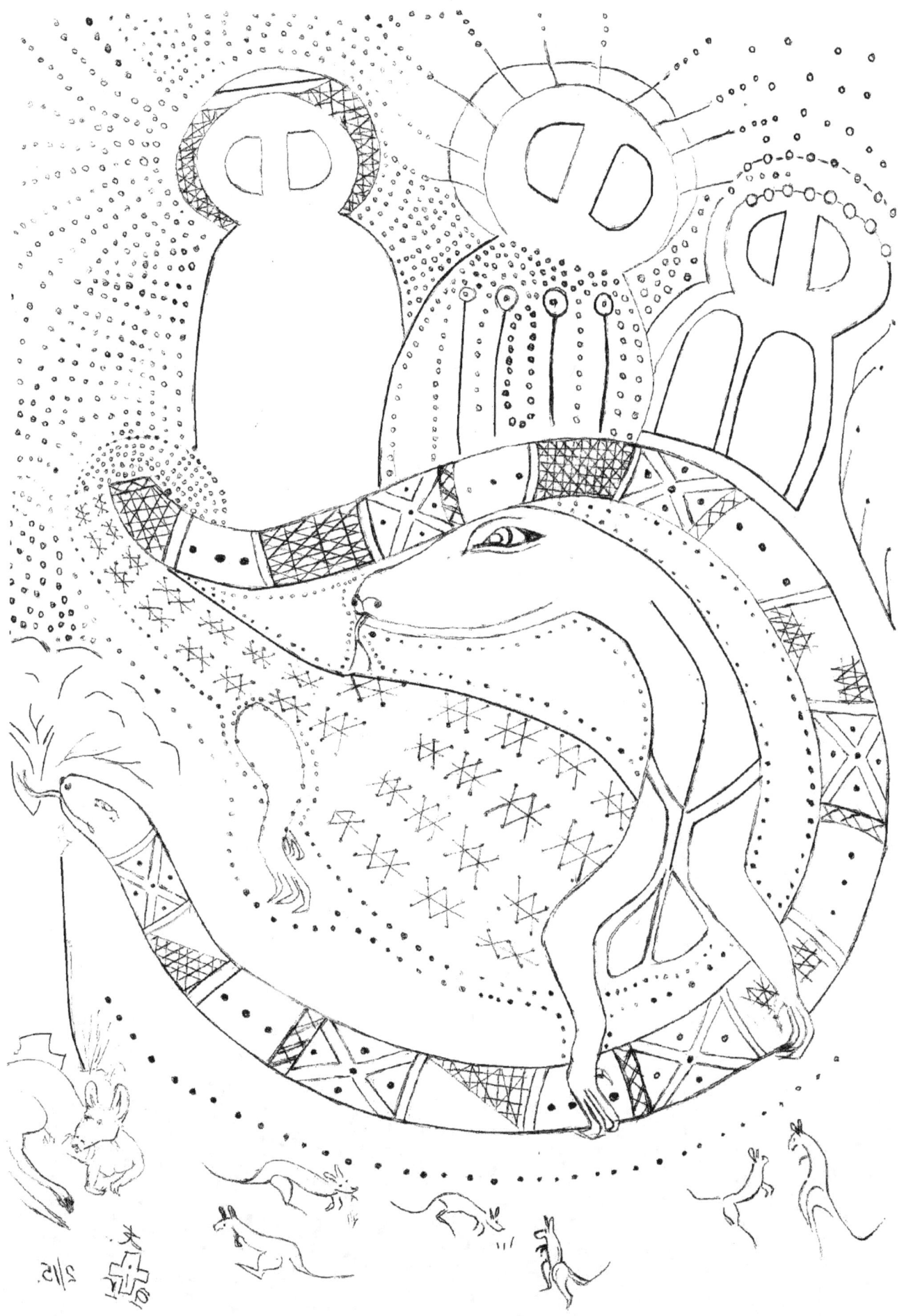

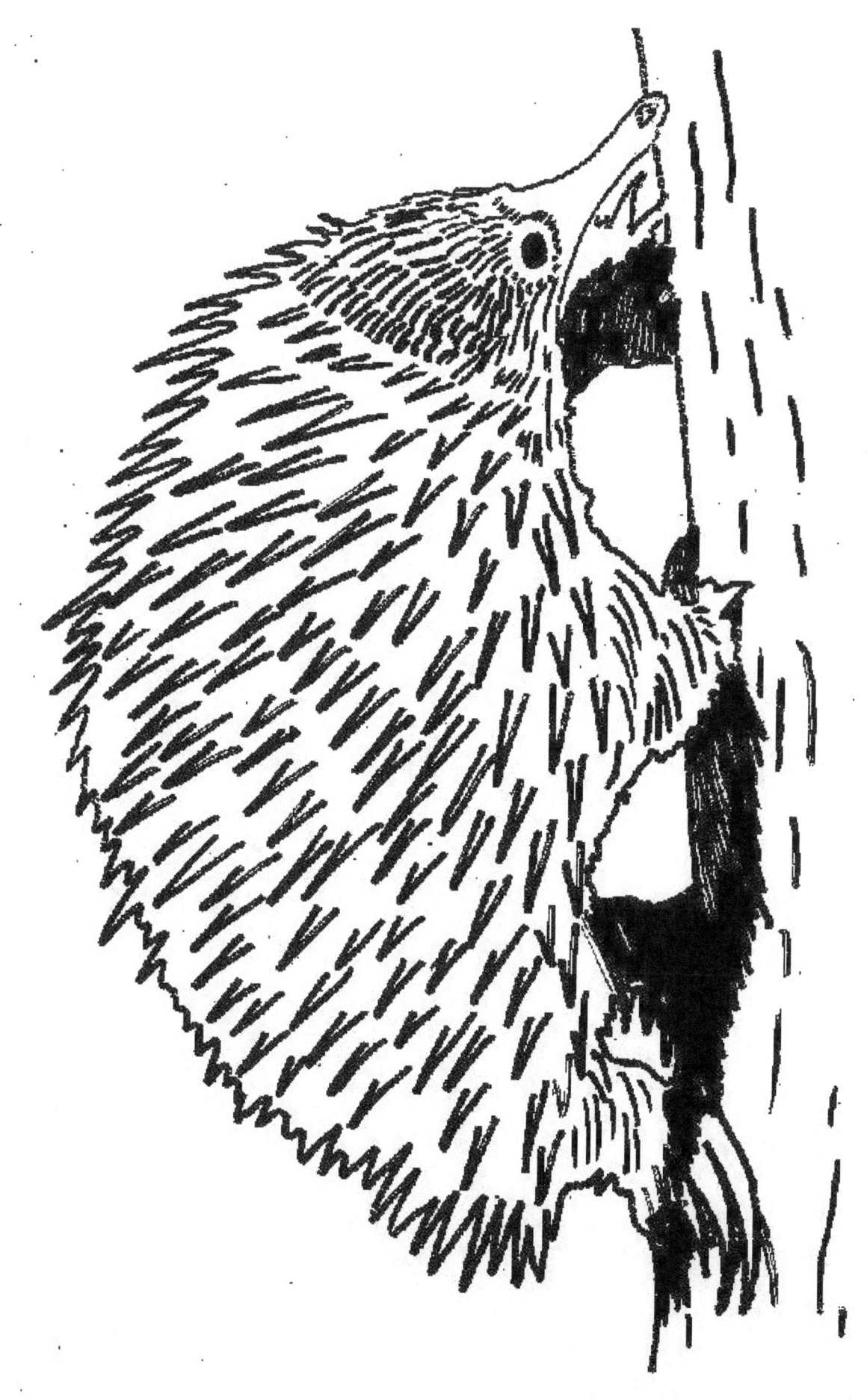

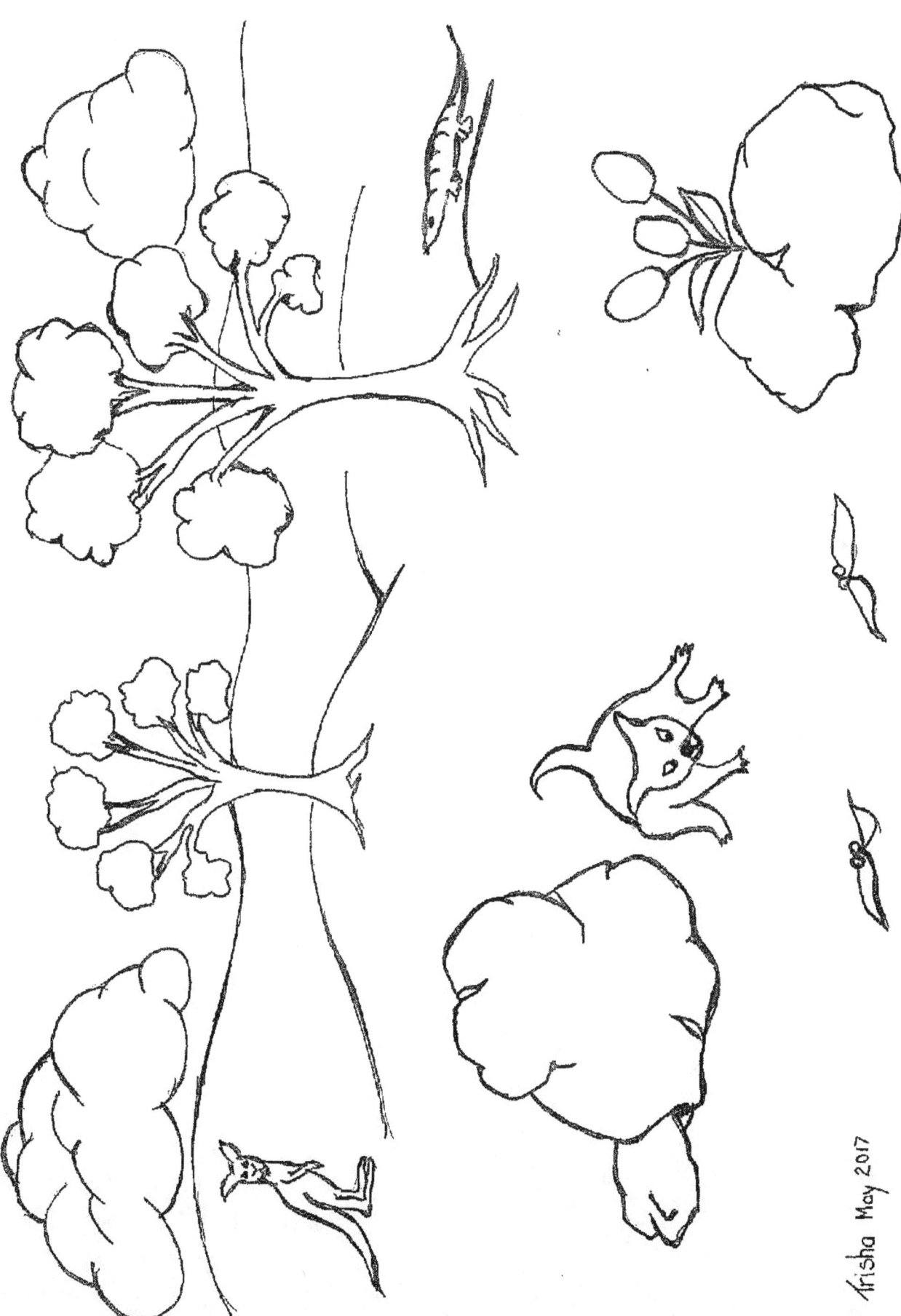

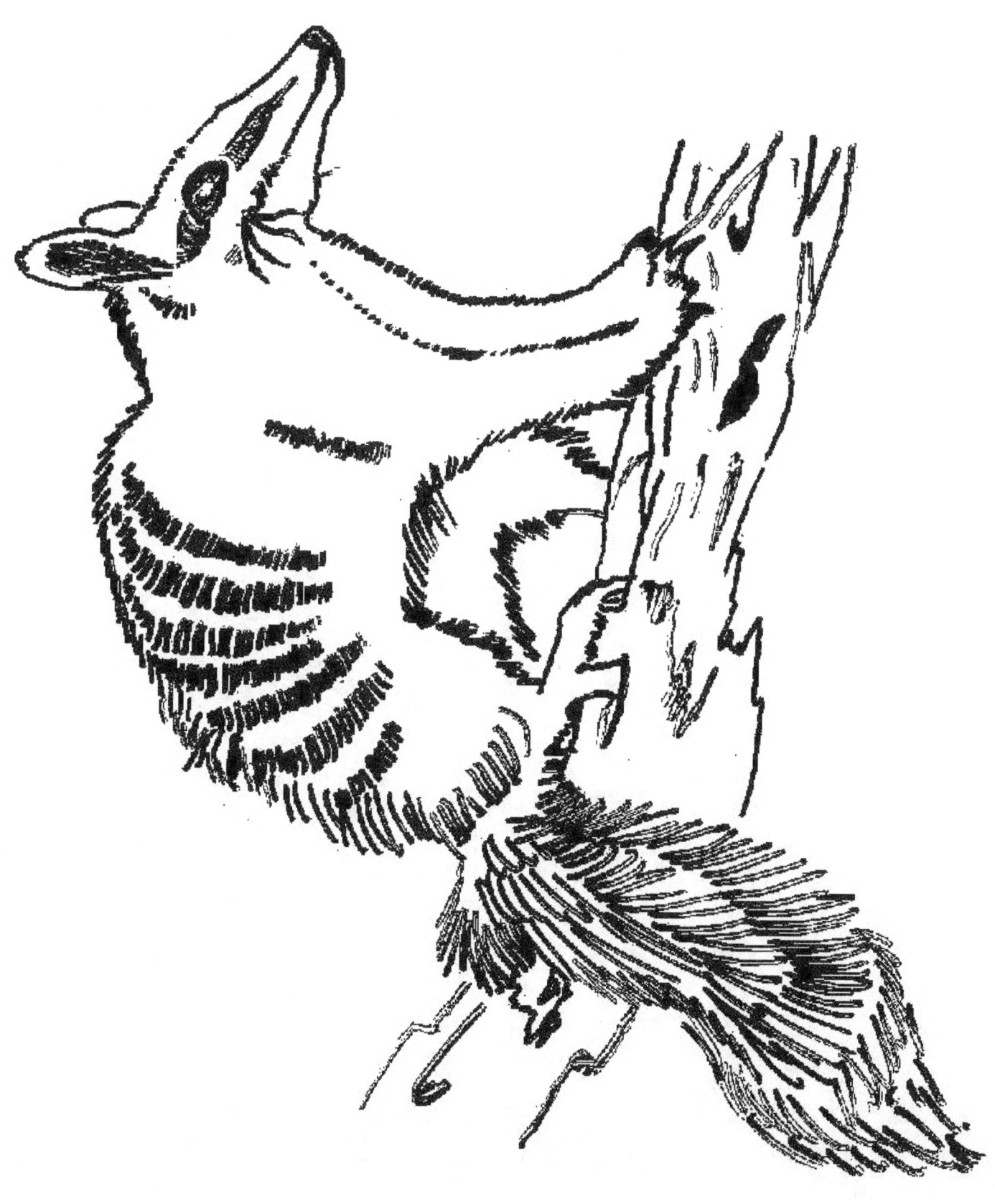

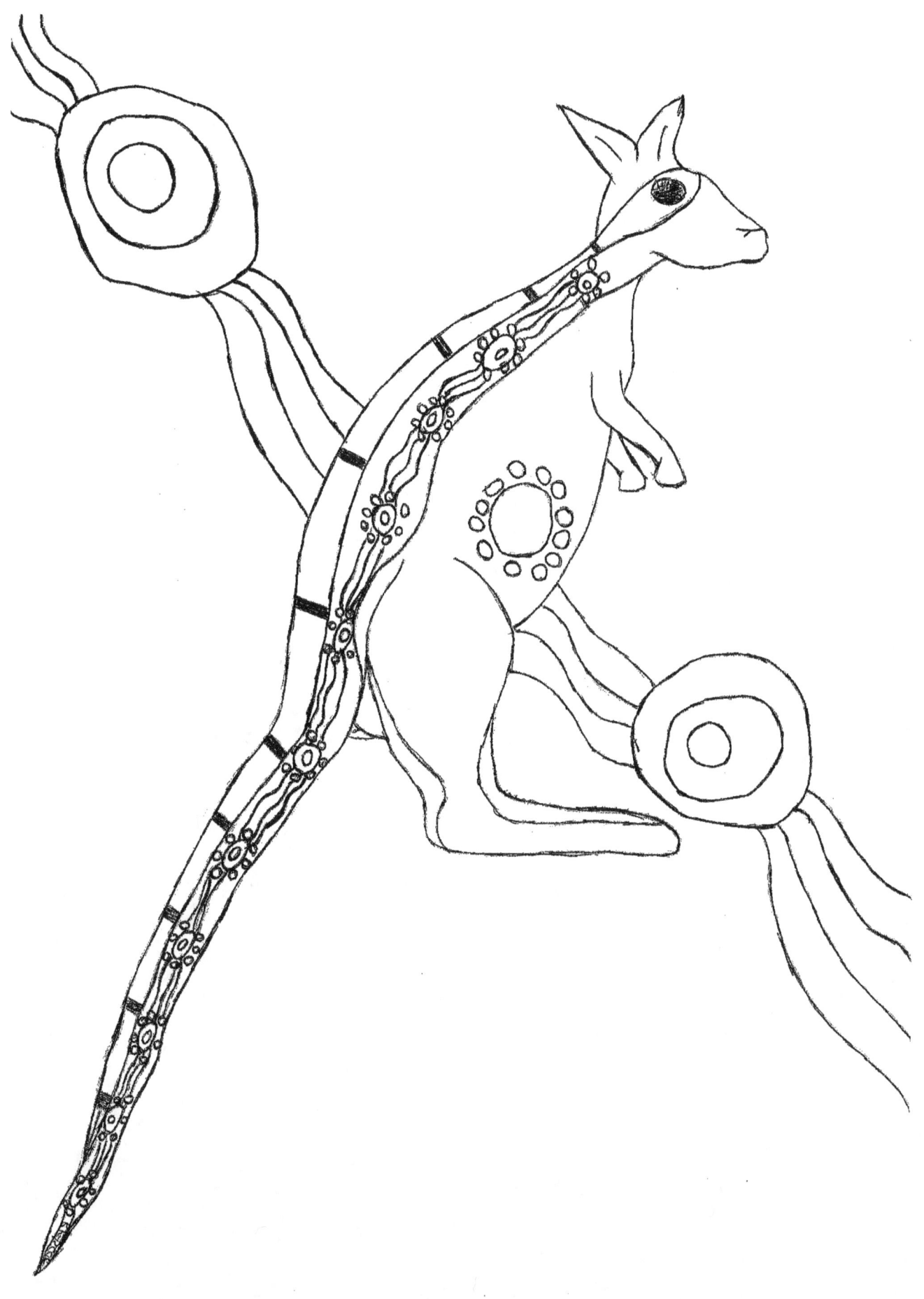

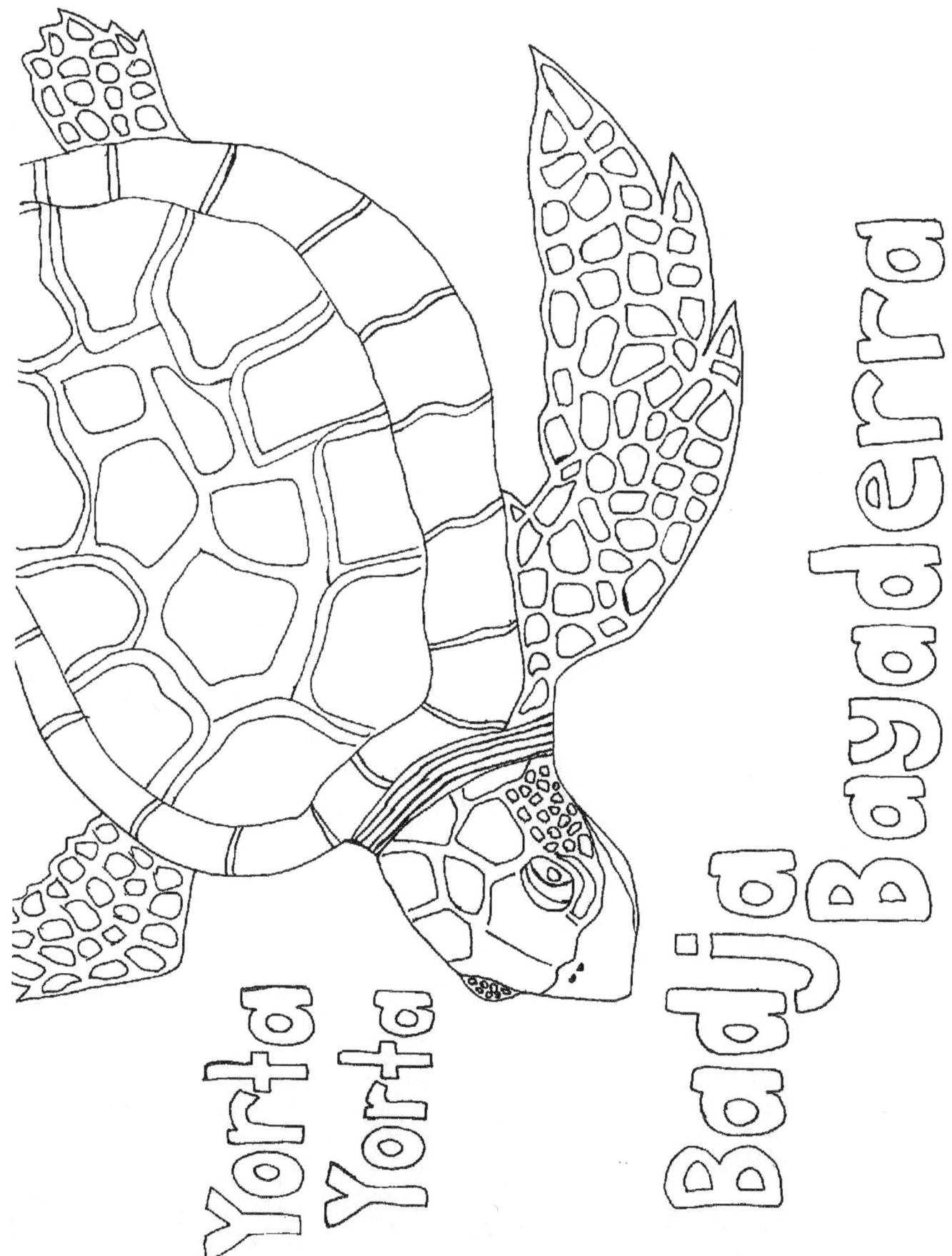

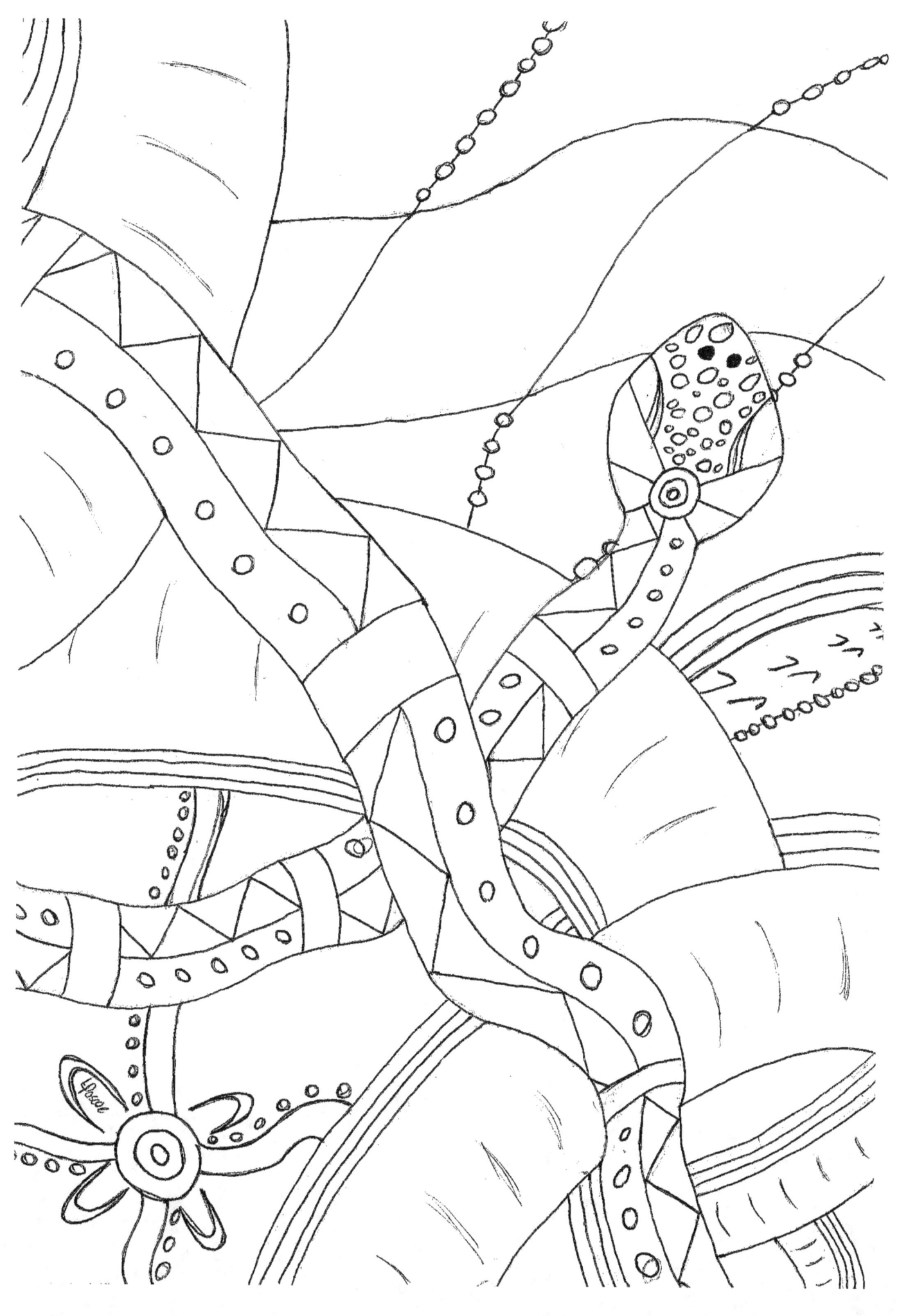

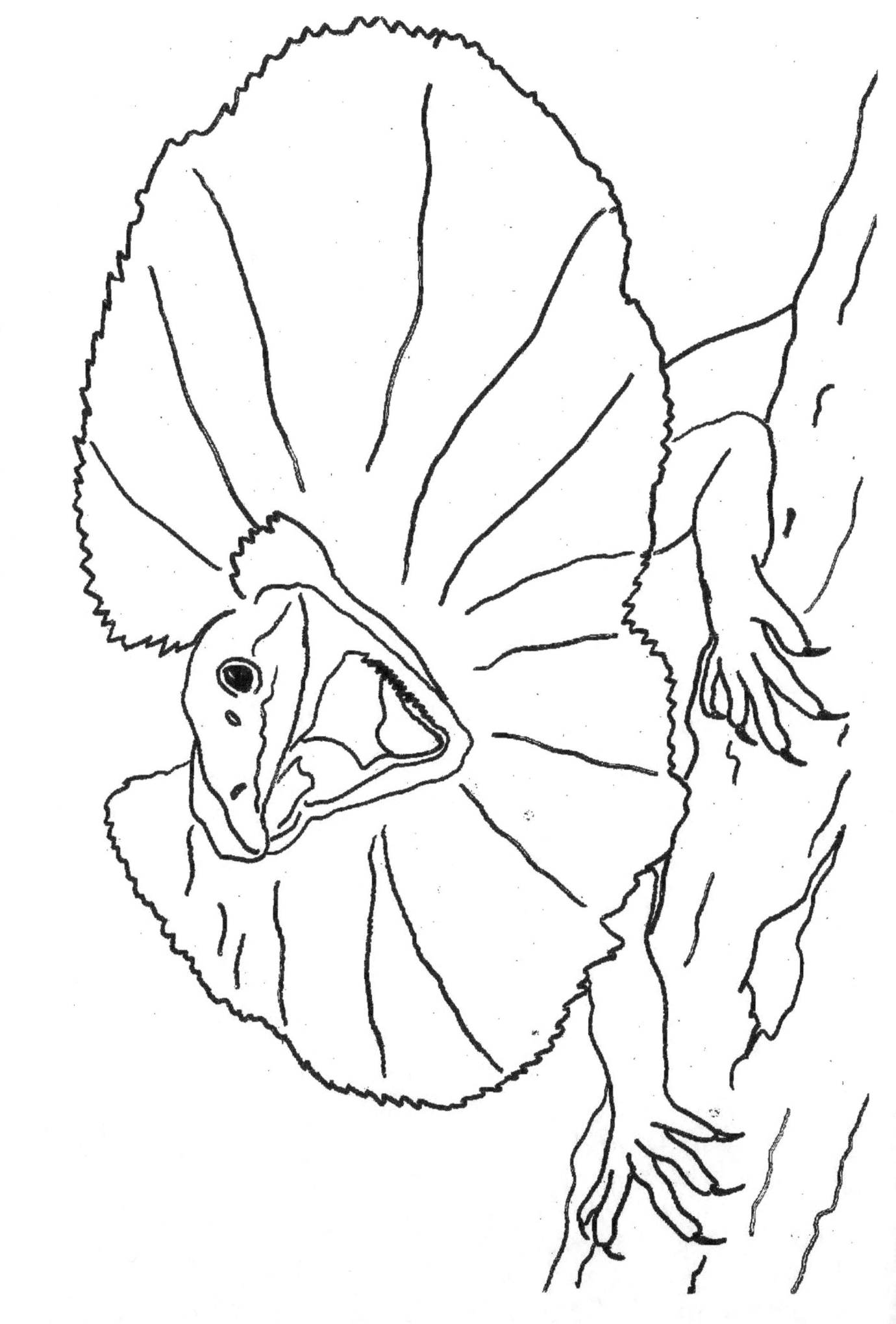

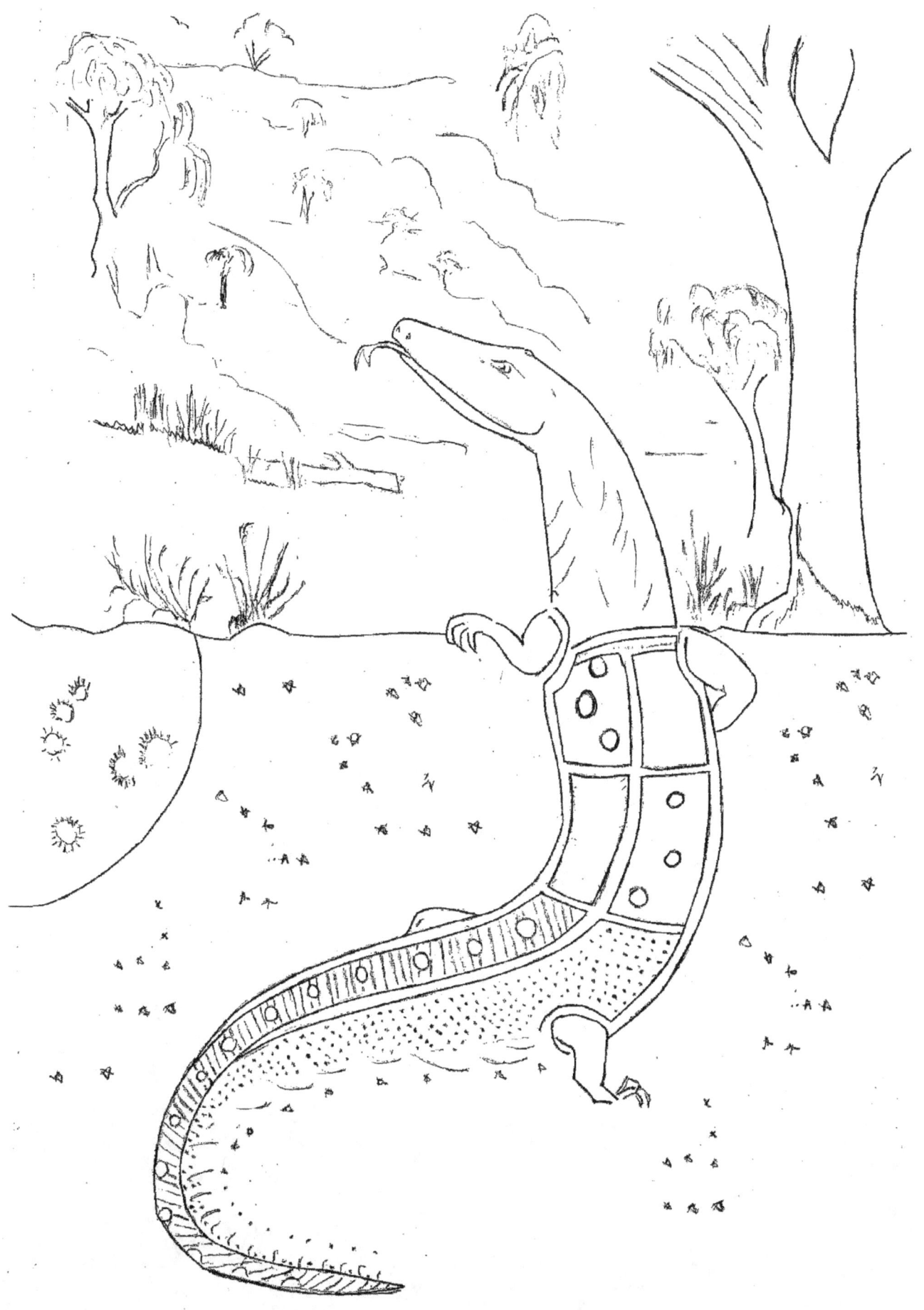

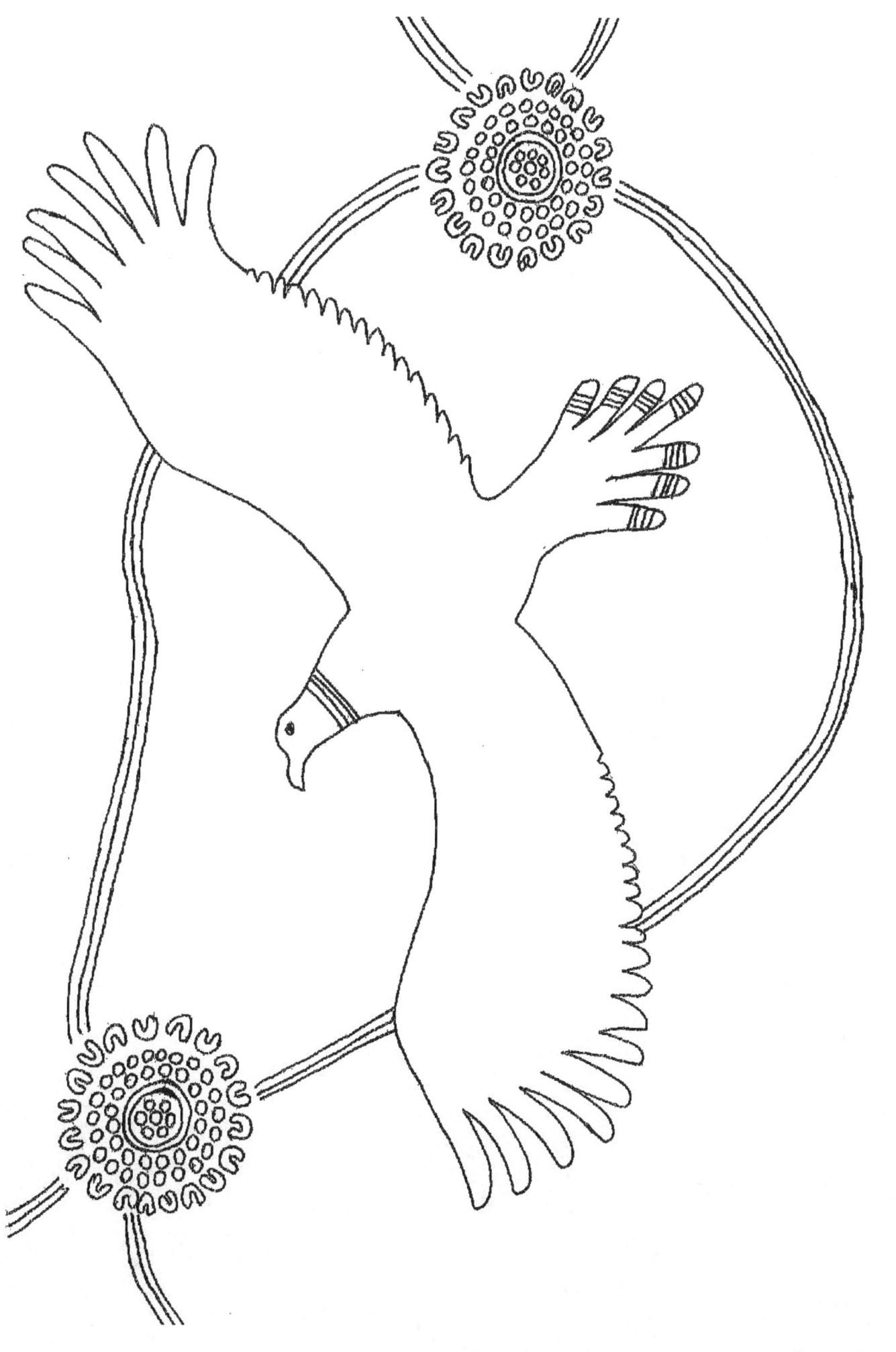

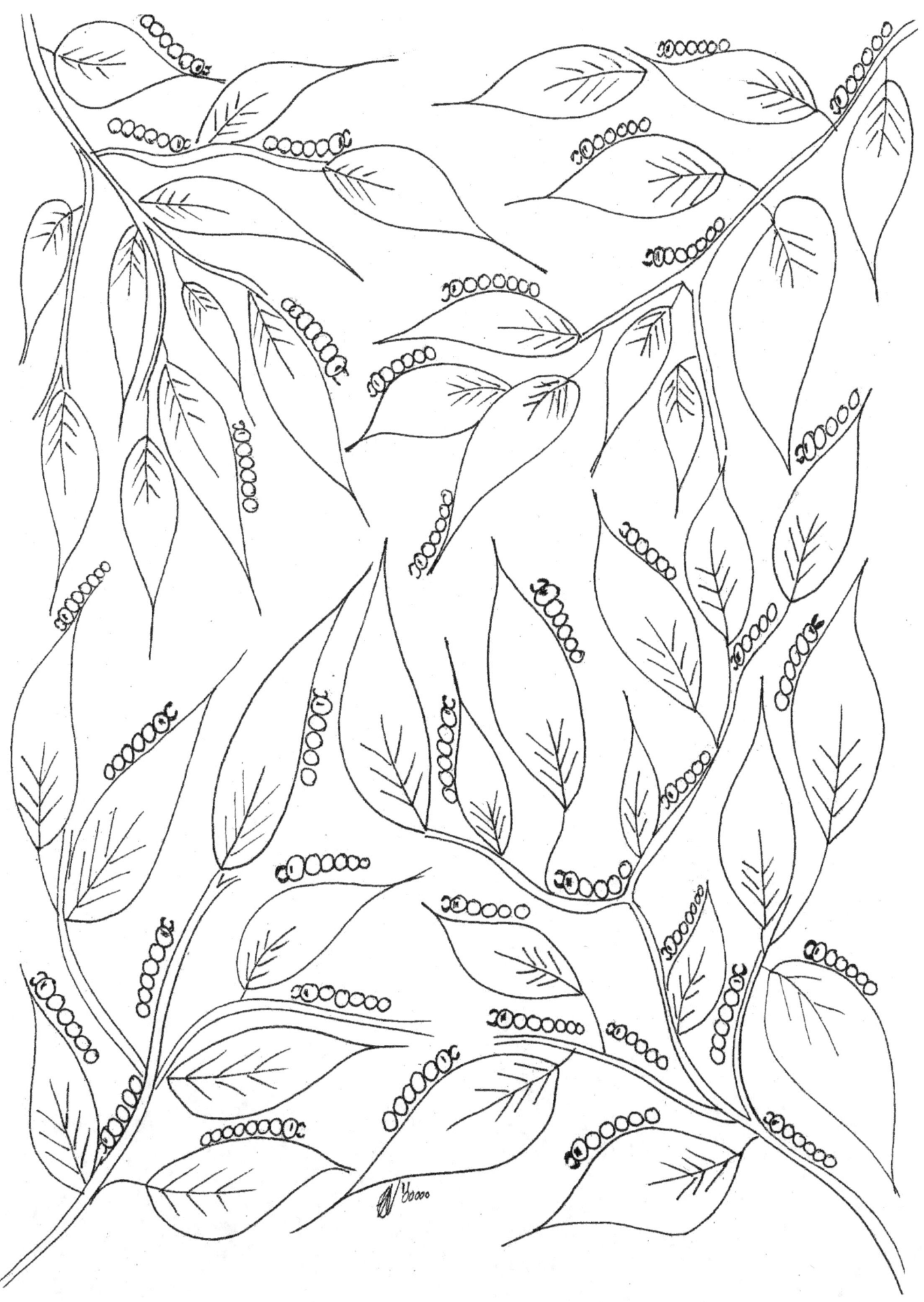

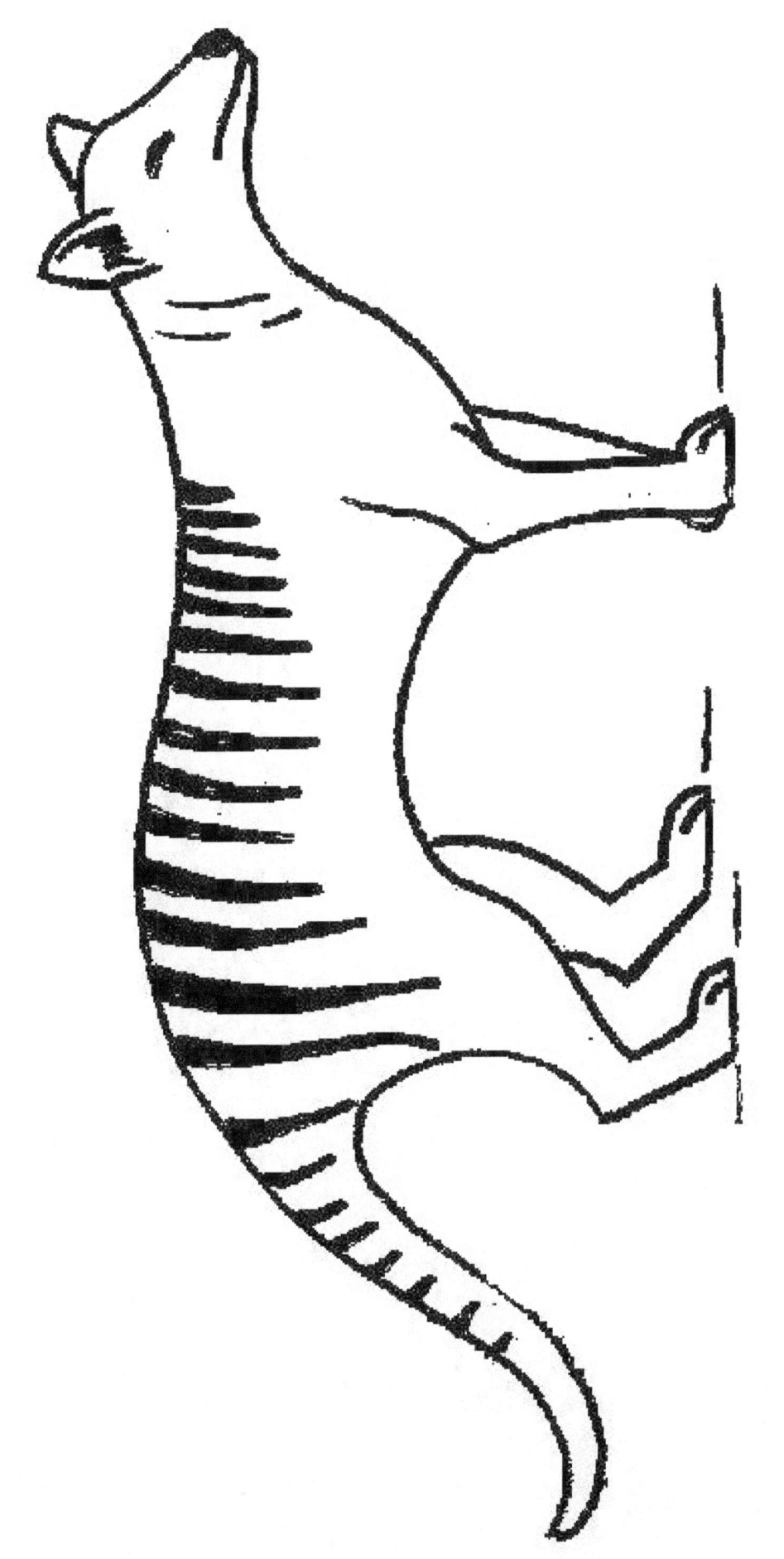

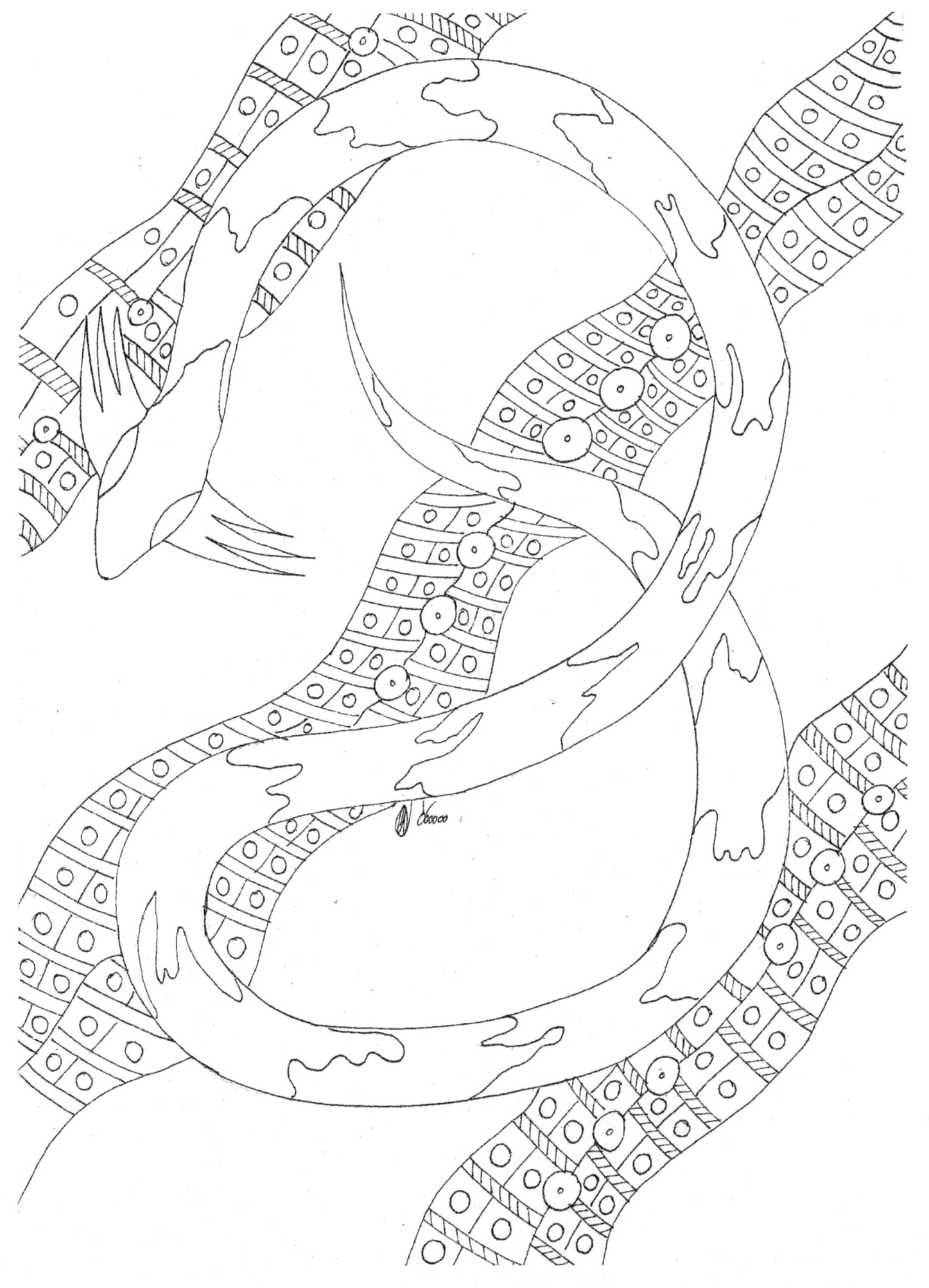

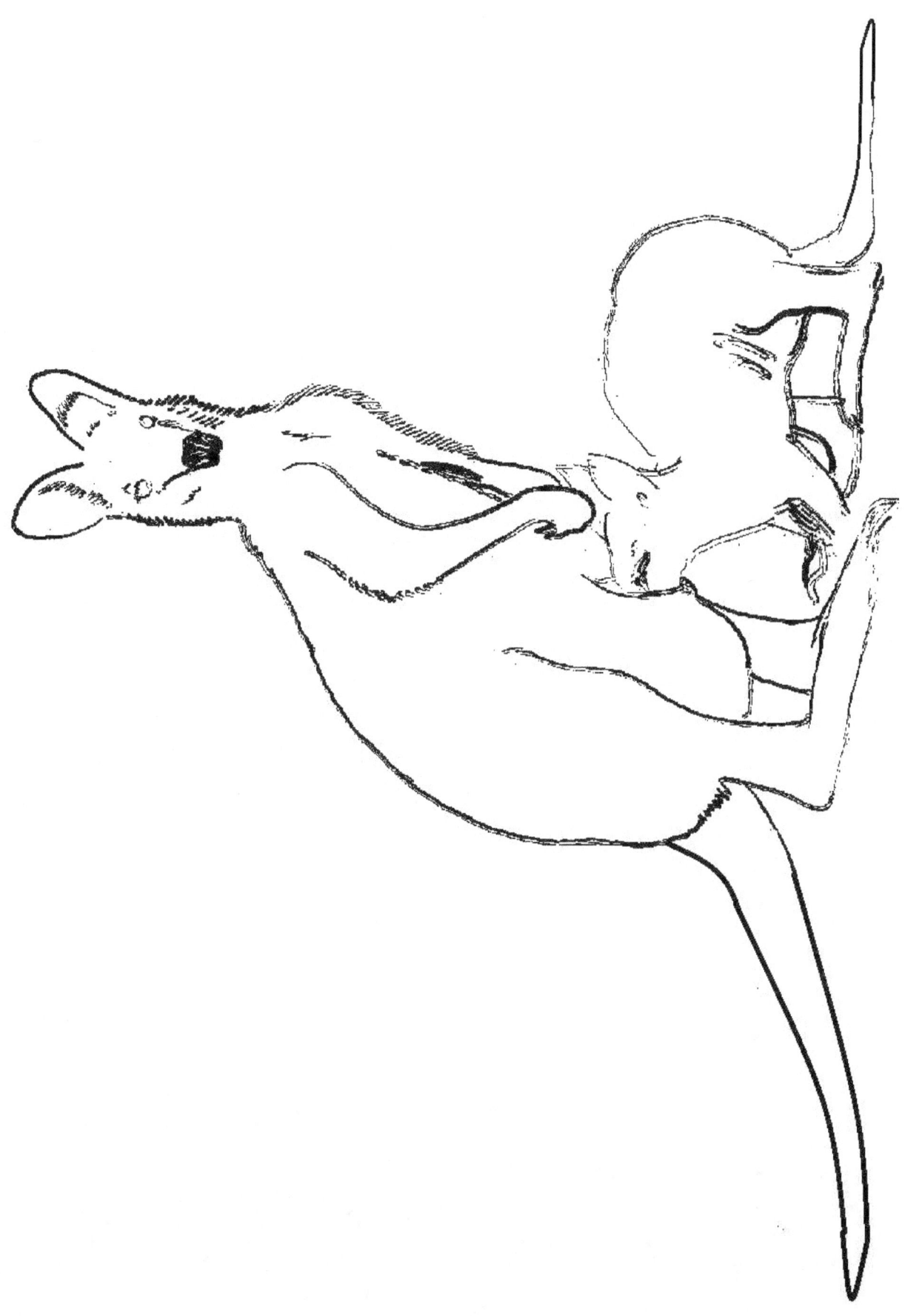

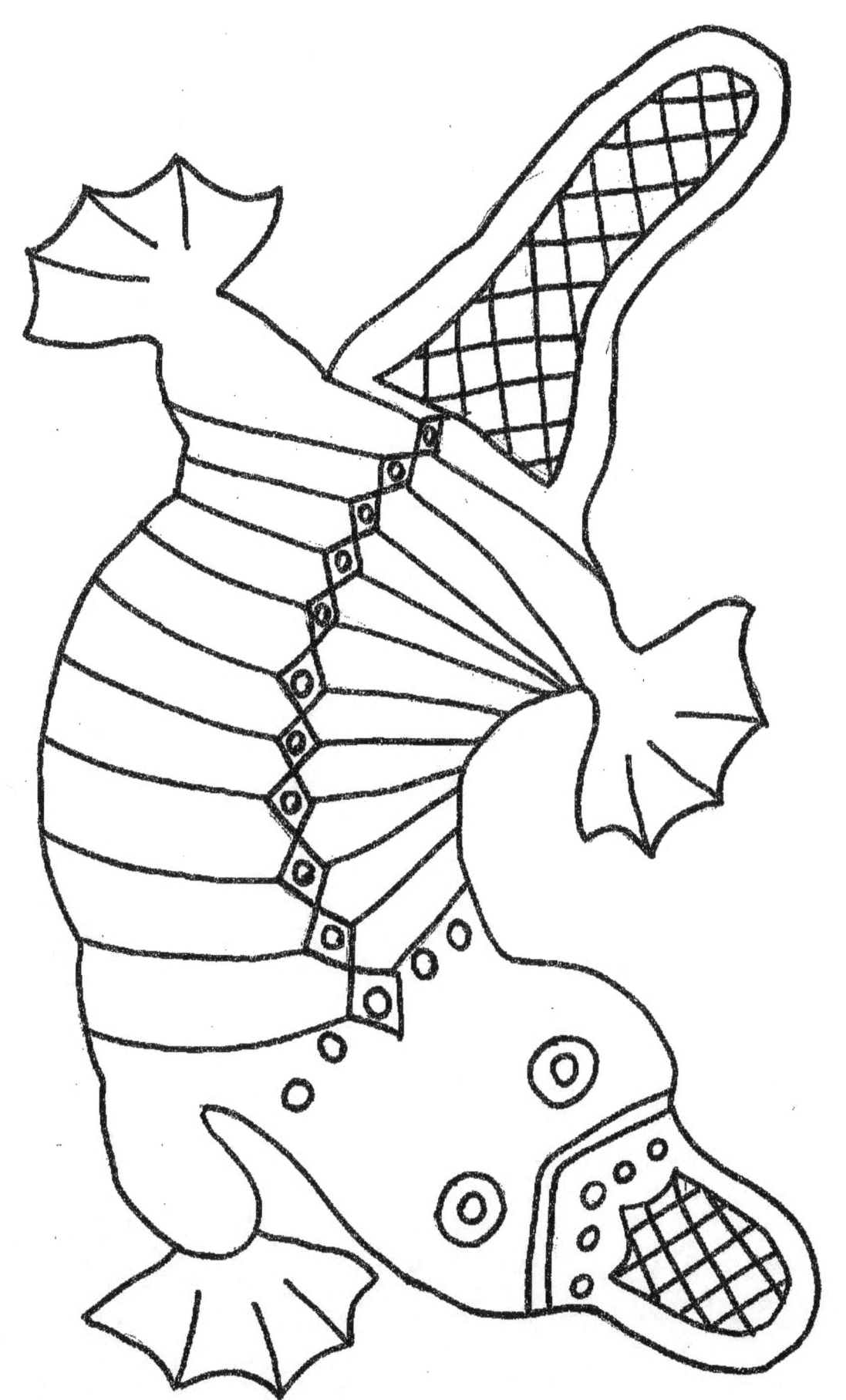

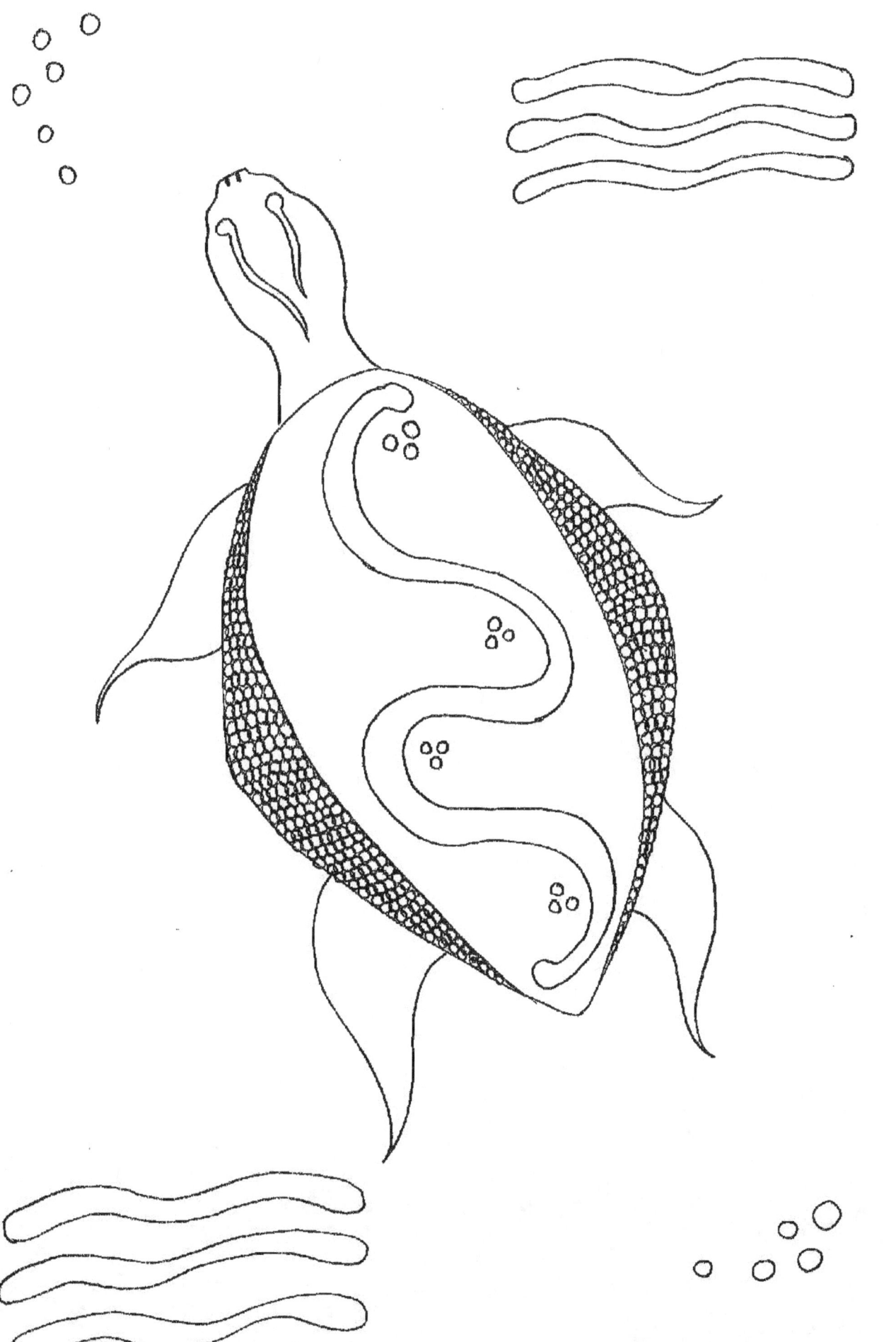

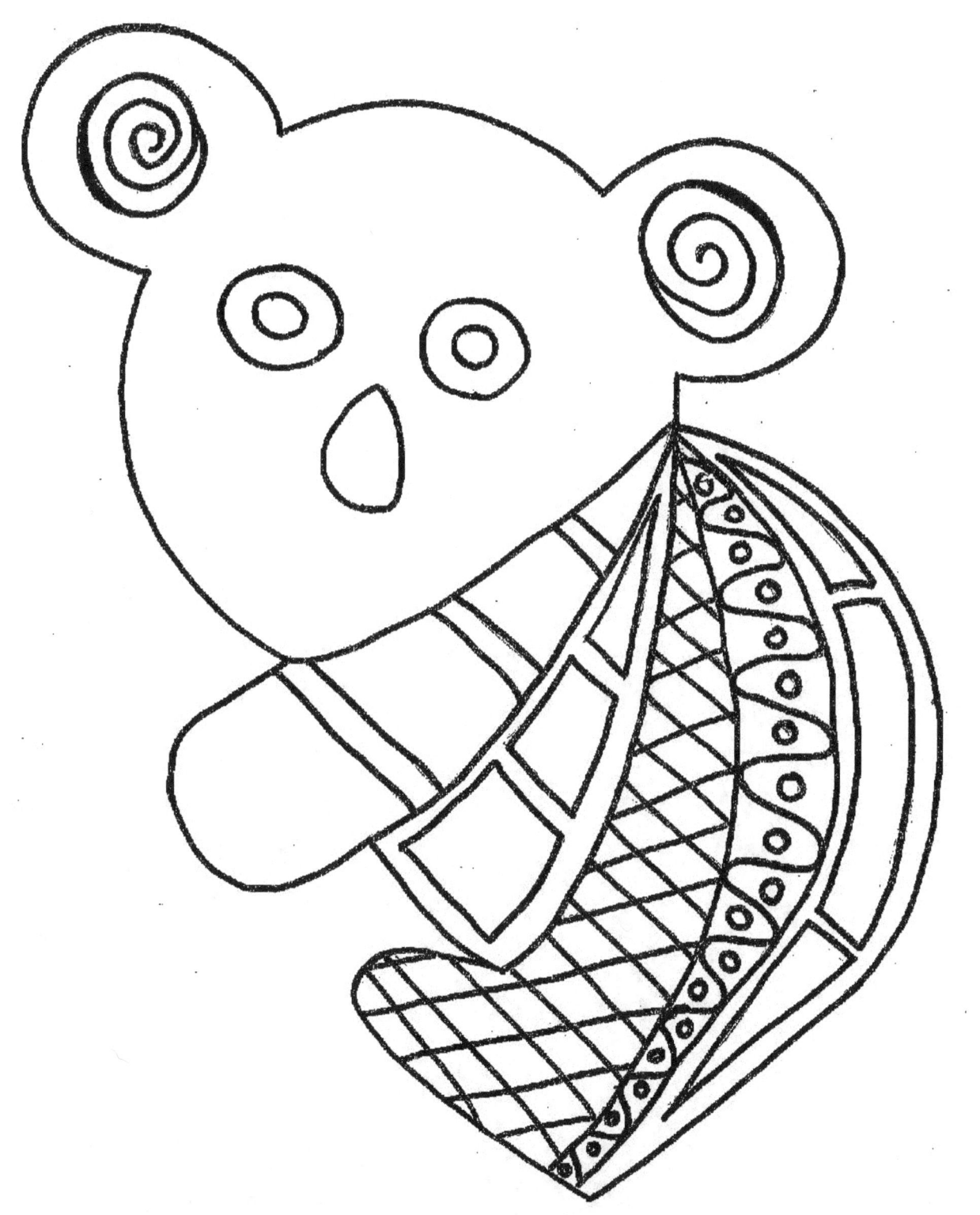

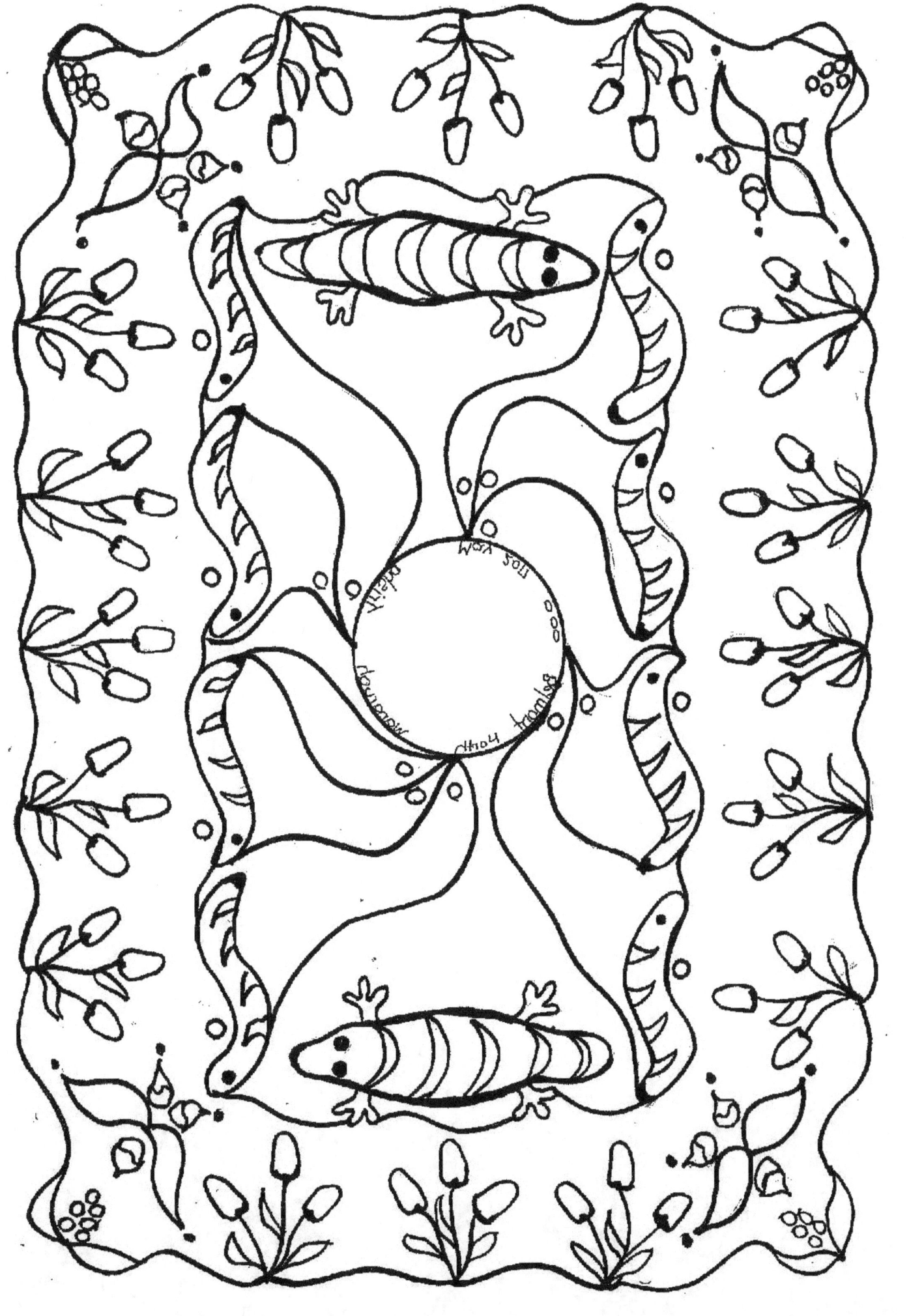

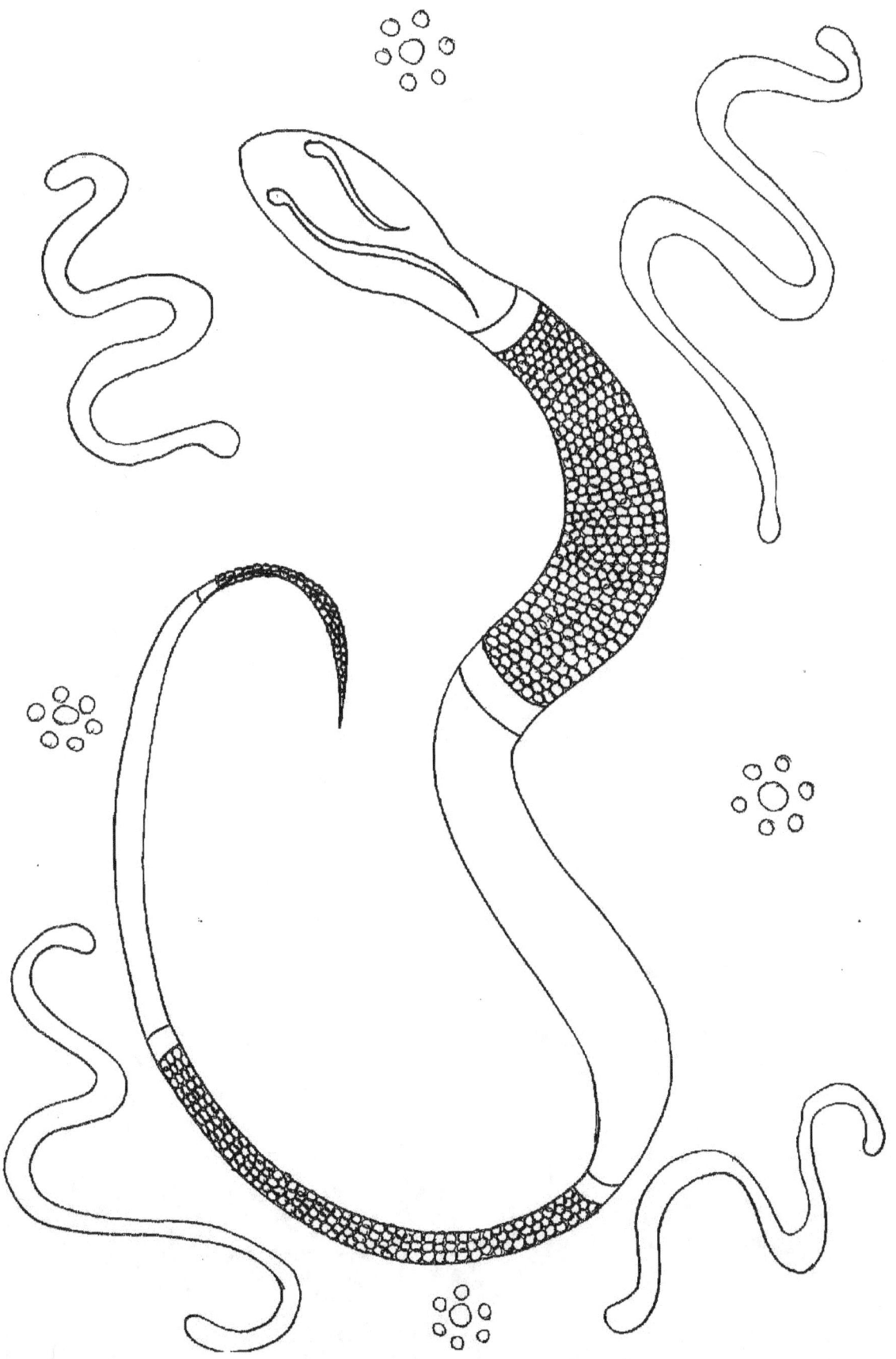

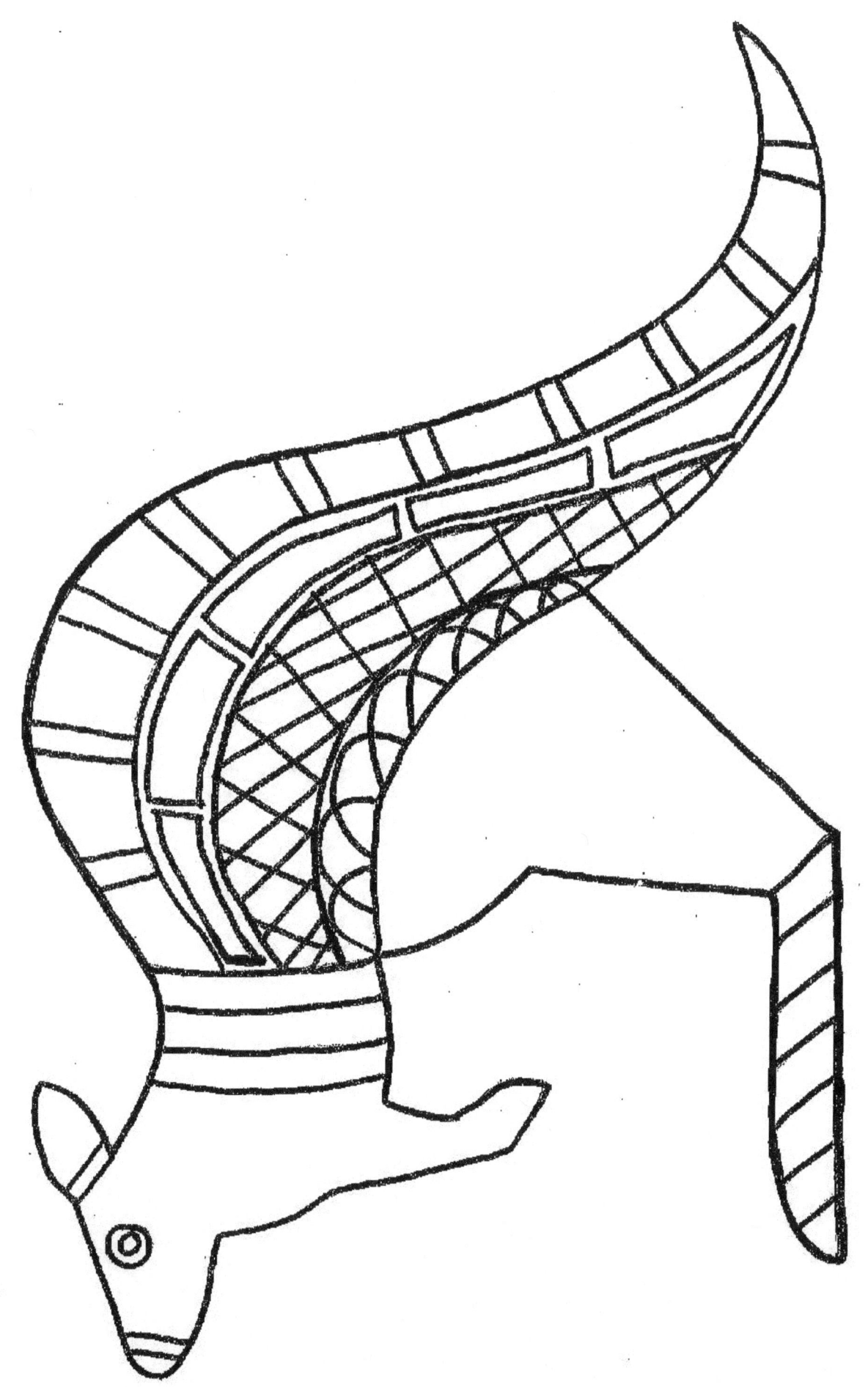

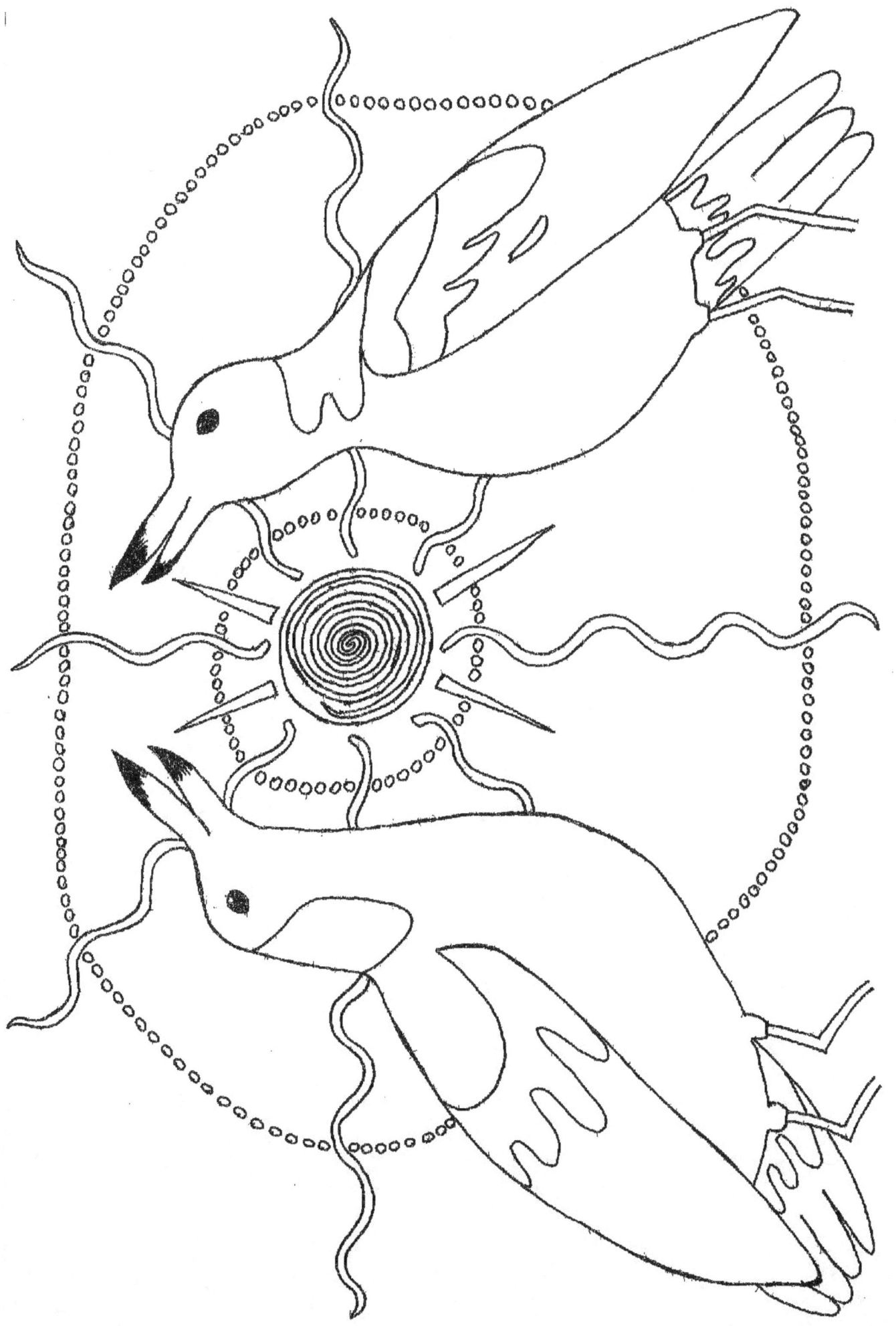

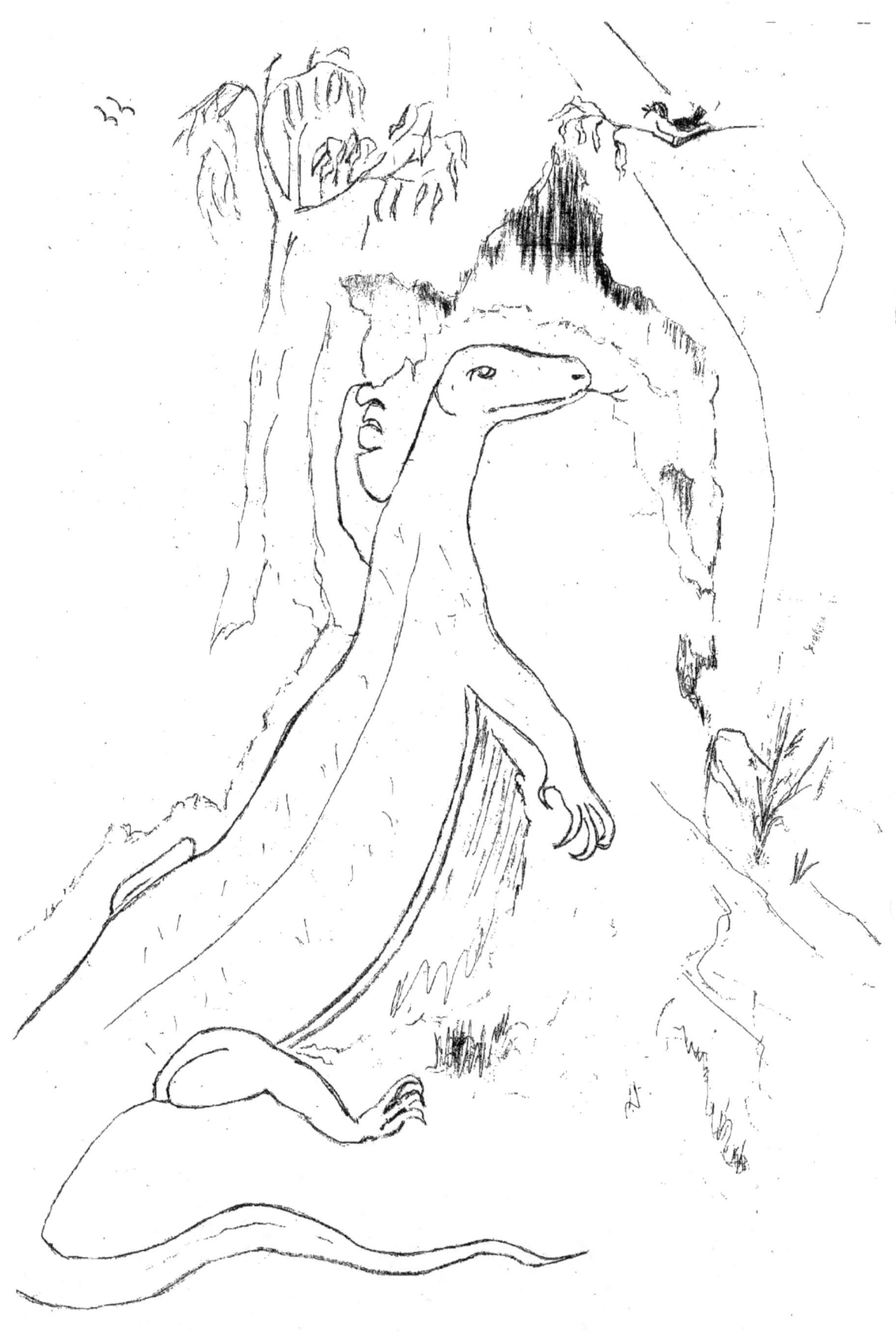

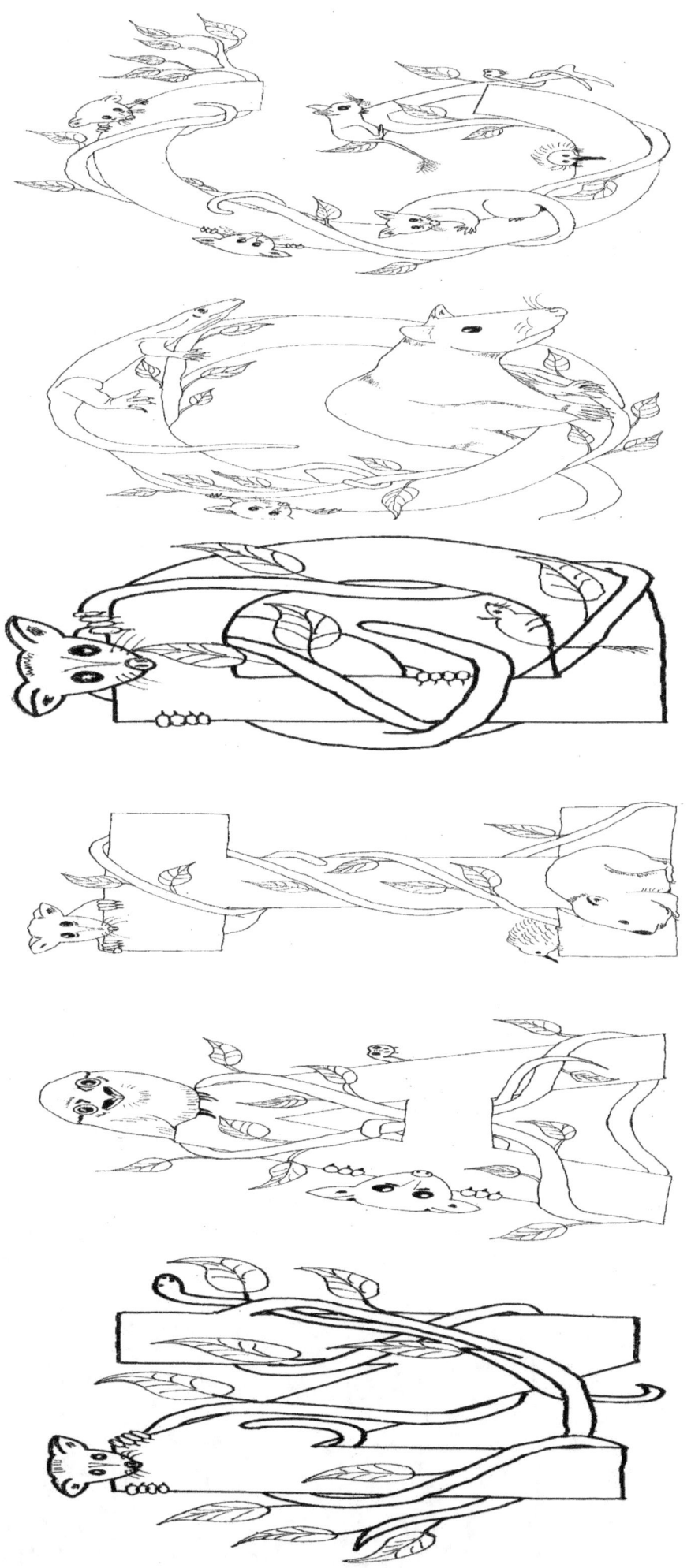

ABOUT THE ARTISTS

Please note some of the Artists did not want to be named. Below are those that allowed us to include their names.

Sharon Dawn Wortley

Dawnie has always been interested in Art and drawing. Initially a self-taught Artist, after completing a Diploma of Fine Arts through the Technical and Further Education college in Gunnedah, Dawnie's first major commission was a work for the first NAIDOC Debutant Ball. She has taught art to the local women's groups and at local schools and for NAIDOC events in Gunnedah. She has taught and inspired others, including a niece and nephew, who follow in her footsteps.

Rosslyn Saunders

Roz Saunders is a Gamilaroi woman and she lives in Muswellbrook and is a member of the Wanaruah LALC. Roz works at a natural health clinic and is a keen gardener.

Renee MacDonald

Renee MacDonald is the administration support officer for the Wanaruah LALC. My job would take twice as long and be much harder without her support. Renee descends from the Bundjalung & Gumbaynggirr people and was raised on Wonnarua land. She is only beginning to explore her artistic side having spent her early years raising and caring for her family.

Bo Jenna

Bo Jenna is 16 years old and Worimi & Yorta Yorta. The drawing of a turtle is the totem of the Yorta Yorta people. Turtle in Yorta Yorta language is Badja Bayaderra.

Alicia Davis

Alicia Davis is a Wiradjuri/Ngiyampaa woman who was raised on Kamilaroi land and has now settled on Wonnarua land to raise her family. She loves to draw and hopes to dedicate more time to it in the future.

Shayne Atkinson

Shayne Atkinson was born in Moree and is a proud Gamilaroi woman. Shayne recently moved to Muswellbrook and regularly drops into Wanaruah LALC for a yarn and to share her latest drawings.

Charlie Towers

The mudcrab "Ghinni was drawn by Charlie Towers. He is 9 years old from Newcastle and belongs to the Worimi people.

ABOUT THE ARTISTS (continued)

Please note some of the Artists did not want to be named. Below are those that allowed us to include their names.

Patricia Laws

Patricia Laws a Wonnarua woman who lives in Belmont North and is a member of the Wanaruah LALC.

Lochlan Pascoe

Lochlan is from the Kamilaroi people of Gunnedah in the North West Slopes Region of New South Wales. At 15 he is an Aboriginal Leader within his school community. Lochlan has an avid interest in performing arts. Along with enjoying art and theatre, he is a keen hockey player.

Kylie Pascoe

Brief: Kylie is from the Kamilaroi people of Gunnedah in the North West Slopes Region of New South Wales. She has a passion for Aboriginal Culture including Aboriginal Astronomy. Kylie has avid interests in neuroscience, sociology and performing arts. Along with enjoying time with her family and community events, Kylie is a keen hockey player.

www.ingramcontent.com/pod-product-compliance
Lightning Source LLC
Chambersburg PA
CBHW082012230526
45468CB00022B/2107